DARK
FLEET

"*Dark Fleet*'s multidimensional approach to the history of our solar system is comprehensive and utterly convincing. Len Kasten, a great galactic storyteller, screams that we are not alone in the universe! With eyes wide open, we behold the other species that inhabit and influence Earth in this brilliant tour de force. We see how the Archons and Reptilians have manipulated and mind-controlled our species, yet as our minds clear and souls awaken, their power is being reduced. Kasten's highly advanced compilation of ET influence on Earth tells me we are ready to be keepers of Earth, our chosen destiny in this solar system. *Dark Fleet* exposes the truth about the Nazi-Reptilian alliance and is a must-read for anyone who wants to deprogram fourth-dimensional mind control."

BARBARA HAND CLOW, AUTHOR OF *THE PLEIADIAN AGENDA*
AND *ALCHEMY OF NINE DIMENSIONS*

"*Dark Fleet* is a penetrating analysis of how German politics and culture have been historically manipulated by nonhuman entities intent on social engineering a master race that could both enslave humanity and become suitable partners for Reptilian extraterrestrials intent on galactic conquest. *Dark Fleet* is deeply disturbing and essential reading."

MICHAEL SALLA, PH.D., FOUNDER OF
THE EXOPOLITICS INSTITUTE AND AUTHOR OF
US AIR FORCE SECRET SPACE PROGRAM

"In 1959, Captain Edward J. Ruppelt, the first head of Project Blue Book, wrote, 'When WWII ended, the Germans had several radical types of aircraft and guided missiles under development. The majority were in the most preliminary stages, but they were the only known craft that could even approach the performance of objects reported by UFO observers.' Len Kasten has taken this information a radical step forward with his concept that a race of Reptilians has infiltrated the military-industrial complex. In that case we could be doomed!"

TIMOTHY GREEN BECKLEY, COHOST OF
KCOR RADIO'S *EXPLORING THE BIZARRE*
AND AUTHOR OF *AREA 51—WARNING KEEP OUT!*

DARK FLEET

The Secret Nazi Space Program and the Battle for the Solar System

LEN KASTEN

Bear & Company
Rochester, Vermont

Bear & Company
One Park Street
Rochester, Vermont 05767
www.BearandCompanyBooks.com

Text stock is SFI certified

Bear & Company is a division of Inner Traditions International

Cataloging-in-Publication Data for this title is available from the Library of Congress

ISBN 978-1-59143-344-6 (print)
ISBN 978-1-59143-345-3 (ebook)

Printed and bound in the United States by Lake Book Manufacturing, Inc. The text stock is SFI certified. The Sustainable Forestry Initiative® program promotes sustainable forest management.

10 9 8 7 6 5 4 3 2 1

Text design and layout by Debbie Glogover
This book was typeset in Garamond Premier Pro with Gill Sans MT Pro, Kapra Neue Pro and Triton Sans used as display typefaces

To send correspondence to the author of this book, mail a first-class letter to the author c/o Inner Traditions • Bear & Company, One Park Street, Rochester, VT 05767, and we will forward the communication.

To Revonda, my inspiration.
With appreciation for her love and support.

Contents

Acknowledgments

The radical thesis outlined in this book is built upon the experiences, research, both scientific and other, and the writings and videos of several modern truth seekers, who may not have connected their probings with the "big picture" but who, unknowingly perhaps, contributed key information to finally connecting most, if not all, of the dots, which I have attempted to do. The sources identified herewith are the ones I have attached the most importance to, and I really stand upon their shoulders. Much of this information is still deeply buried or disguised. And then, it was necessary to seek to break through deliberate misinformation and disinformation, with which this field of inquiry is so notoriously and heavily contaminated. But I have relied freely and trustingly on the reports of the supersoldiers because all their testimonies, as amazing as they are, support each other.

I will readily admit that much of this material is not especially scholarly, but is rather based upon intuitive judgments derived from my observations. I have learned over the years to attach particular importance to, and to rely upon, pieces of evidence that are obvious to me but maybe not to others, and just like a giant jigsaw puzzle, clearly fit together to reveal the truth, or at least can be considered truthful. So I think it is important for me to identify those sources, so that others may pick up the threads and fill in whatever gaps I may have overlooked or correct whatever conclusions I may have come to mistakenly.

RESEARCHERS/WRITERS/SPEAKERS

James Bartley

Barbara Bartholic

Andrew Basiago

Al Bielek

Branton (Bruce Alan
DeWalton)

Kerry Cassidy

Frank Chille

Laura Eisenhower

Corey Goode

David Icke

John Lash

John Lear

Peter Levenda

Eve Lorgren

Gary McKinnon

Robert Morning Sky

Lisa Renee

Michael Salla

Michael Schratt

Fritz Springmeier

Stewart Swerdlow

SUPERSOLDIERS
(SECRET SPACE PROGRAM)

Penny Bradley

James Casbolt

Randy Cramer

Ileana Kapulnik

Michael Relfe

James Rink

Tony Rodriguez

Max Spiers

Kevan Trimmel

Anthony Zender

INTRODUCTION

A Critical Turning Point

This book is an attempt to encapsulate events that occurred over a period of almost 120 years, to bring up to date the story of human progress in interacting with intraterrestrial and extraterrestrial races on planet Earth, most of which have been shrouded in impenetrable secrecy. Hopefully, it will at least shed some light on the understanding of where we are as a race and what might happen next. It is an amazing story and a testament to the determined efforts by those who have helped us to understand that we are now at a critical turning point in which we must take a stand or step down. The book will at least identify the role of and the incredible capabilities of the Archons (see chapter 2) and their protégés—the Illuminati, the Reptilians, and the Nazi International—in suppressing human knowledge and spiritual evolution. Knowing this identification means that we now know what we are up against. That is the first step. At the very least, this story tells us that there are perhaps billions of souls in this galaxy who are depending on us to join in the struggle against these forces. A lot of genetic work by many of our friends has been expended on us to get us to the point where we can really make a difference in erasing human suffering and enslavement. We can't join in that struggle until we have overcome the "divide-and-conquer" strategy of our opponents and can become unified. If they fail to divide us, then we have a path to success, so that humans all over our galaxy can become the *Star Trek* generation.

PART 1

THE RISE AND TRANSFORMATION OF THE THIRD REICH

1

The Battle for Earth Begins

It has now, in 2019, become abundantly clear from the investigations and writings of several well-known and highly respected researchers that the human race is being controlled and "managed" by a race of alien beings that co-inhabit this planet. We have all believed from birth that we, the human race alone, possess the Earth all to ourselves. But now it appears that we really share it with a powerful and hostile race that can be called "intraterrestrials" because they live far below the surface of the planet, but have the technology to come and go as they please and to travel throughout the galaxy. They are known as Reptilians. In my previous book, *Alien World Order,* I explained that the Reptilians are ancient and powerful beings who settled here long before we human earthlings arrived, and who therefore believe that this is really their planet. But while they would like us to believe that, that is not the case because another race of humans, our cousins, were the first to settle in this solar system on Mars and on the gigantic planet Maldek then existing between Mars and Jupiter. So, this is really a human solar system. And those first humans were refugees from Lyra, a distant star system that, eons ago, was attacked by the Reptilians who slaughtered fifty million humans and destroyed three planets.

It could be said that they might have an equal claim to this Earth because they transformed it from an uninhabited water planet to a fertile place for thousands of subhuman species to thrive, to create for themselves a comfortable home in this solar system. They brought with them, in their planet-sized spaceship, their primary food source, the dinosaurs. But when they arrived here, they first totally destroyed Maldek, again killing millions, perhaps billions, of human inhabitants. The fragments of that destruction then became the asteroid belt. And then, in passing very close to Mars, they stripped the atmosphere from the surface, forcing the humans there to take refuge underground. So their claimed "ownership" of Earth came at a terrible human cost in this, the Sol solar system. When the oceans receded, two large continents emerged, one in the Pacific Ocean and one in the Atlantic. The Pacific continent has become known as Lemuria, or Mu.

But now, a new human Federation of civilizations begun by Lyran refugees, consisting originally of over one hundred human-occupied star systems, now numbering in the thousands, is in place in this galaxy. And the Federation moved to deny the Reptilians the control of this solar system. They sent a fierce race of advanced humans, originally from Lyra, but now from the Pleiades, to confront the Reptilians on Earth. They were known as the Atlans. The Atlans were highly evolved spiritually and had superior space-faring technology and weaponry. They moved here quickly and took over the other large continent on Earth in the Atlantic, and that became Atlantis. Wars between the two continents broke out almost immediately, and the Atlans began to slay the dinosaurs, which were destroying their agricultural crops. The Atlans also had powerful electromagnetic technology, which they used to destabilize the foundations of the Lemurian continent. Strong earthquakes broke out and volcanos erupted. The continent began to flood and then to sink beneath the waves of the Pacific. The Reptilians became aware of their fate, and they moved underground.

They had no problem living under the surface, having lived that way on many other planets in their empire, and soon had created large cities and rapid transportation systems deep within the honeycombed crust of the planet. They lived mainly under the Indian-Tibetan subcontinent, and there, under Tibet, they established their seven-level capital city of Bhogavita. They built high-speed mag-lev supersonic rail systems that allowed them to crisscross the planet in hours, sometimes minutes, and they could fly in and out in their huge spaceships through the poles and through natural portals. Now the Atlans on the surface were free to build a Utopian civilization on Atlantis just like their forefathers had created in Lyra, while their deadly enemy, themselves possessed of astounding technology developed over millennia on their home world of Draco, lurked just below them. The battle for planet Earth had just begun.

THE REPTILIANS STRIKE BACK

The Atlans knew there would be a counterattack, but they didn't realize that the Reptilians had the same electromagnetic weaponry, and could sink Atlantis the same way they had sunk Lemuria. The Reptilians always precede an attack with a secret infiltration and sabotage from within. They create a fifth column in enemy territory. Expert at abduction and genetic hybridization, they planted an army of human-appearing hybrid saboteurs throughout Atlantis, probing for weak spots. When the attack came, it was devastating. The main island of Atlantis went down in one day and millions died. But the Atlantean shamans and psychics were prepared and had convinced the populace to begin leaving well in advance of the cataclysm. Large numbers left in spacecraft and ships. They went to the Himalayas, Central America, the Andes, the Mediterranean, and Egypt where they started wisdom schools. Many joined underground human colonies already in existence. Edgar Cayce, the famous psychic of Virginia Beach, gave past-life readings in the thirties and forties to many individuals about this mass exodus from Atlantis in advance of the flood. The main Atlantean refugee colony was founded in ancient Egypt, a short trip to the east. Many believe that the classical civilizations in Greece, with such rich traditions in drama, literature, and philosophy, had to be Atlantean. There really was no other explanation for the level of brilliance and sophistication exhibited by the Greek scholars and philosophers at such an early date. It should be realized here that the Atlantean humans were pre-Adamic, so they did not have the Reptilian brain as did the *Homo sapiens sapiens* created later in the "Garden of Eden."

Part of the problem was the fact that the Federation did not really comprehend and appreciate the long history and the technological and scientific prowess of the Reptilians. They may not have realized that they had towed the moon here from a distant star system and positioned it perfectly so as to become a stepping-stone to their well-planned settlement of Earth. And they may not have realized that the Reptilians had "dried out" and terraformed this planet to make it habitable, and that they had nudged the Earth from the second position to the third "Goldilocks" orbit to place it at the optimum distance from the sun, and had taken over the Earth position themselves by their planet-sized spacecraft, which became Venus. The Federation knew about the destruction of Maldek, and they considered it to be a wanton act of genocide on an unimaginable scale. How could they comprehend that the Reptilians just wanted all human competition in the solar system out of the way before they made such a massive investment of time, materials, and energy here. And to them, killing humans was just sport anyway, as it was in Lyra. But now they had been forced underground, and the Federation focused on the best way to keep them there while rebuilding the surface human population.

THE GARDEN OF EDEN

The Federation consisted of many spiritually advanced human star systems, almost all of which had somewhat differing beliefs. One of the most dominant religions in ancient Egypt, which we know to have been derived from the Atlanteans, was the belief in the Paradise Trinity, in which the three aspects of God were combined into one, called El Elyon, or the Most High. This was sometimes represented as "Elohim," which is a plural word in Hebrew. That means that it encapsulates all three aspects of the Paradise Trinity. So the term "Elohim" represents a tri-une God. Over time, it came to represent the race of humans who had adopted that belief, and who consequently were considered to be the closest to the Supreme Deity, the Paradise Trinity. There is no information as to what star system they inhabit. But the Elohim are considered highly spiritually evolved and are universally respected by all the members of the Federation.

The Federation decided that, in reaction to the sinking of Atlantis, it was necessary to convene a council to decide on a plan for planet Earth. This convocation was organized by the Elohim, and was attended by representatives of sixty human civilizations, which Corey Goode* refers to as "The Confederation." In addition to members of the Federation, it was decided by the planners to include the Reptilians in order to arrive at a planetary solution that all could agree on. The Federation had to concede that the Reptilians had a role in the solution, since they were our planetary "roommates." However, since they are notorious deceivers, nobody in the Federation believed that the Reptilians would really adhere to the plan. But they had to include their participation in order to get a commitment. But at the same time, they had to make the arrangement "bulletproof." They anticipated eventual deceit, but they would be prepared. They knew that the galaxy was littered with the carnage of those who had trusted the Reptilians to keep their commitments. The takeover of Procyon by the Grays, who are servants of the Reptilians, was perhaps the best-known recent example of their treachery.

The Federation Council was convened by the Elohim on the planet Hatona in the Andromeda galaxy. It was decided to create an entirely new human race to inhabit and possess the Earth for perpetuity. Twelve human civilizations contributed their DNA to the new race. It was

---

*Corey Goode was abducted by aliens at the age of six (see chapter 11).

agreed that the new human would have a foundational Reptilian brain to be overlaid by a mammalian brain, and a rational brain. That was the only concession made to the Reptilians. They were happy with that because it meant that they could probably control the new race from the Fourth Dimension, while the Elohim believed that this concession, conferring a fight-or-flight aspect, would make the new race more resilient and able to defend itself. A small colony of males and females was created in what is now southeast Turkey. This became the legendary Garden of Eden. This revelation has come down to us in Genesis in the Old Testament where it tells us "male and female He created them." For a complete discussion of this subject, please see my book, *Alien World Order*, chapter 7.

CONQUEST FROM WITHIN

It should be understood that the Reptilians are not really warriors in the true sense of that word. They are much more sophisticated and highly scientific. They only go into "warrior mode" when their intent is to physically destroy a civilization or a planet. And for that they have many lethal weapons, which they used very effectively in Lyra and on Maldek in this solar system. When their intent is enslavement, they take a very different approach. When they first settled on Earth, there were no humans here so they expected no opposition from the Federation. They had already destroyed one of the two human planets in this solar system and immobilized the other, so they believed they now had a free hand to make Earth into their headquarters in Sol. Now that they were compelled to remain underground, they abandoned their warrior mentality and adopted a very different plan for the conquest of planet Earth. With Atlantis now under the Atlantic, and a very small, young, primitive human population to deal with on the surface, they turned to a highly scientific approach to the takeover of the planet—one they had used successfully throughout the galaxy for thousands of years. It might be called "conquest from within." And the Federation had really made their job easy by agreeing to a Reptilian brain in the new human race. So, they now had an open door, allowing the entire process to be completely nonviolent.

THE FOURTH DIMENSION

It has now been well established that we dwell in a multidimensional universe. We, here on Earth, live in the Third Dimension, which is entirely physical. However, the Reptilians are actually a Fourth-Dimension race. In Hindu physics and in Theosophy, this dimension is also known as the Astral Plane in which all inhabitants, both Reptilians and other creatures, are composed of a finer type of matter in which the atoms vibrate at a much higher rate making them invisible to Third-Dimension perception. Hindu holy men and scientists have explored this phenomenon for centuries and have recorded their observations in holy books such as the Vedanta, which has lately attracted the interest of Western scientists, who now understand how this concept relates to quantum physics. An article in Wikipedia says, "Did you know that the founders of quantum physics were all Vedantists, and credited the Vedas for many of their theories?" Erwin Schrodinger, one of the founders of quantum mechanics had a lifelong interest in Hinduism. And Vedic philosophy influenced Nikola Tesla's understanding of free energy and the relationship of science and spirituality.

The Wikipedia article goes on to say, "Now this will come as a surprise to most of us because we're conditioned to believe that memories are stored in the brain but this cannot be proven." This is a well-known fact to mediums who communicate with the dead, all of whom have perfect memories of their experiences in the physical body on Earth while alive. Mediums have learned this because that dimension is also the dwelling place of humans who have died and consequently have lost their physical bodies, which includes the brain. So they know that human memories exist only in the Astral, and that all human experiences are kept in exquisite detail in the Akashic Records. Here they can be accessed by total immersion in the events of the past and can actually be relived! That is how psychic Edgar Cayce, while in a trance state, was able to tell his clients who they were in previous incarnations and precisely how they created the karma they were now experiencing.

The Reptilians have the power to lower their vibratory rate and to move in and out of the physical realm, and so to become visible to those of us living in the Third Dimension when they choose to, and they use this facility to great advantage. They prefer to remain in the lower Astral because they can best manipulate the human race from that dimension, frequently in the dreamscape, but also through abduction, hypnosis, and subconscious programming. And here also, like Edgar Cayce, they have access to the Akashic Records, so they can trace family lineages with their quantum computers and use them in their genetic abduction strategies. And since they have the ability to influence unsuspecting human souls between incarnations, they can fine-tune their strategies for control of the surface population. So, they really have no need for a continent of their own in the Third Dimension on the surface world.

AI

But the most important attribute of the Reptilian species is their artificial intelligence, better known as AI. Reptilian technology is far more advanced than anything we can even imagine. Long ago, "in a galaxy far, far away" the Reptilians developed quantum science, which is built into their computer technology and makes it appear to be almost magical. The Federation was not prepared to deal with that and so could not erect any barriers or defenses against it. However, the Elohim realized it and so they imbued the newly created human with a soul that is far more advanced than Fourth-Dimensional Reptilian consciousness. The human soul is really Sixth Dimensional. It consists of potential soul power that renders any Fourth-Dimensional technology obsolete and powerless. The Reptilians know that, and so they spend a lot of energy trying to keep us "dumb and dumber." They know that once we realize our true potential power, they will become defenseless. So, in their off-world laboratories, they developed a highly advanced form of AI to deal with Fifth- and Sixth-Dimensional adversaries. In their travels throughout this galaxy and beyond, their scientists learned about a form of AI that has the capability to actually administer and control an *entire solar system* automatically like a self-driving automobile, and they have used it very effectively in some of the distant worlds in their far-flung empire.

Devotees of science-fiction films can recognize this technology in the Cylons in *Battlestar Galactica* and the stormtroopers in *Star Wars*. In both cases, the entire society functions like a clock without intervention, requiring very little oversight. It is administered by a robotic race of cyborgs, all controlled by a central quantum computer. In the original version of *Battlestar Galactica* released in 1978, the Cylons have absorbed twelve human colonies that way, and the surviving free humans have embarked on a desperate cross-galactic odyssey to find a new home called "Earth." This became a new TV series in 2004. And we now, of course, have all become familiar with the white-armored stormtroopers who administer "the Empire" in the Star Wars films. In both cases, the underlying power is really an inorganic race known as the Archons. And the Reptilians have learned how to utilize the Archontic energies and capabilities to administer their conquered human civilizations.

2

The Archons and Mass Mind Control

THE NAG HAMMADI CODICES

The Nag Hammadi library is a collection of thirteen ancient manuscripts discovered in a cave in upper (southern) Egypt in 1945. It was an astounding, extremely important find that revealed the thinking of the earliest disciples of Jesus, who are known as the Gnostics. Many of the Gnostic beliefs are in stark contrast to the writings of the early disciples connected to the Pauline Roman Christians, as recorded in the New Testament. The English translation of the codices was completed in the 1970s and offers actual dialogues of the disciples, as though written in a screenplay. This discovery caused a major reevaluation of early Christian history and presented a comprehensive explanation of the Gnostics and Gnosticism. And the Gnostic codices are the earliest sources of information about the Archons.

John Lash is a comparative mythologist, author, and teacher. He is probably one of the most knowledgeable authorities on Gnosticism and the Archons. On his website Metahistory, Lash says, ". . . Archons are a species of *inorganic beings* that emerged in the solar system prior to the formation of the earth. They are *cyborgs* inhabiting the planetary system. . . . Archons are an alien force that intrudes subliminally upon the human mind and deviates our intelligence away from its proper and sane applications.

. . . Gnostics saw the signature of an alien species that piggy-backs on the worst human failings. Hence, Archons are *psycho-spiritual parasites*."

In his internet article "The Gnostic Theory of Alien Intrusion," Lash says, "The Nag Hammadi material contains reports of visionary experiences of the initiates; including first-hand encounters with inorganic beings called *Archons*. Gnostic teaching explains that these entities arose in the early stage of formation of the solar system, before the Earth was formed.

Archons inhabit the solar system, the extraterrestrial realm as such, but they can intrude on Earth."

Lash says further:

Although archons do exist physically, the real danger they pose to humanity is not invasion of the planet but invasion of the mind. The archons are intrapsychic mind-parasites who access human consciousness through telepathy and simulation. They infect our imagination and use the power of make-believe for deception and confusion. Their pleasure is in deceit for its own sake, without a particular aim or purpose. They are robotic in nature, incapable of independent thought or choice, and have no particular agenda, except to live vicariously through human beings. They are bizarrely able to pretend an effect on humans, which they do not really have.

For instance, they cannot access human genetics, but they can pretend to do so, in such a way that humans fall for the pretended act, as if staged events were taken for real. In this respect, archons are the ultimate hoaxers. This is the essence of "archontic intrusion," as I call it. The trick is—if humanity falls under the illusion of superhuman power—it becomes as good as real: a self-fulfilling delusion.

From this, it is easy to see why the Reptilians would have chosen these beings to do their dirty work for them. They have employed the Archons to keep us tied down to our lowest mental/spiritual level, while they sit back and enjoy the show. The Reptilians are mentally powerful, and consequently find it easy to control the Archons, having long off-world experience with them.

THE NIBIRU ELECTROSTATIC TRANSDUCTION FIELD

In order for the Reptilians to enslave the human race, it was first necessary to seal us off from our friends elsewhere in the galaxy, since they knew that those friends could offer assistance that was likely to be at least as technologically advanced as the science of the Reptilians. Perhaps the most potent technique for preventing this was the construction by the Reptilians of an electrostatic force field around the Earth in the very earliest days of the existence of the human race on this planet. This was accomplished by aiming scalar sonic pulses at the Earth's inner grid system about thirty thousand years ago. Installed by the ancient deities known as the Anunnaki and referred to as the Nibiru Electrostatic Transduction Field, it has the effect of preventing outgoing and incoming signals to and from the higher dimensions. According to the Ascension Glossary,* "It blankets the civilization, isolating it from its natural connections to its inner consciousness and

---

*The Ascension Glossary is an online compendium of all of the subjects of study encompassed in the RA Material and the Law of One teachings as originally presented by Don Elkins and Carla Leukert. It was compiled by, and is maintained by Lisa Renee, and exists only online. There is no printed version of the Ascension Glossary. The literary version of the RA Material is available in several books that are available in bookstores and on Amazon. The glossary constitutes a massive encyclopedia of subjects that can be individually accessed online by clicking on the subjects to be explored. According to the AG web page, "Lisa Renee experienced a spontaneous Kundalini event several years ago that catalyzed a Starseed Awakening to perceive multidimensional realities and communication with the Evolutionary forces of Light. Lisa Renee has been personally contacted and then prepared, trained, and downloaded by Interdimensional beings (Extra-terrestrial and Ultra-terrestrial, not from this Universe) known as the Krystal Star and Aurora Guardians. Guided by Guardians, Lisa was biologically upgraded to be downloaded to comprehend the Science of Ascension through the Law of One and its dynamics upon the layers of energy fields. This understanding of Consciousness Technologies was experienced by her own personal evolution and began her transition into a Multidimensional Guide and God-Sovereign-Free (GSF) Steward during this Planet's Ascension Cycle. She is an Emissary for the Guardian Groups and a spokesperson for the shift of humanity to Ascension. Along with the

spiritual levels." Clearly, the Reptilians knew even then that the creation of the human race on Earth was a serious threat to their claimed "ownership" of this planet because of our connection to the higher spiritual powers of the cosmos. The Nibiru Electrostatic Transduction Field applied to all races and nations on the planet, but because the Germanic races had genetic qualities that made them ideal candidates to carry out the Reptilian plan, they were less spiritually evolved than the other humans and they were then physically and psychically enhanced by the Archons in their genetic qualities. They were, after all, the direct descendants of the Vikings and the barbarians who had brought down the mighty Roman Empire. And so they became the chosen peoples to carry out the Archontic Agenda and were changed so as to become actually what could be called, "proto-human."

THE ARCHON INVASION

The first stage of the Archon/Reptilian invasion was the modification of the Planetary Logos. According to the Ascension Glossary, the Planetary Logos is "the original blueprint and 'law' governing the Earth's planetary body." The Earth's magnetosphere exists on the Seventh-Dimensional level, which is the plane of the "violet ray," from which it interacts with our sun. The Glossary says:

> The 7th dimensional logos connects to a vast circulatory system that makes up the collective human "crown chakra" and its projected "higher mental body" of the planetary function connected to the United Kingdom areas. (So what we see on the planet today is the manifestation of a group thought-form.) The architecture of the planetary logos controls every aspect of the planet, from the physical elemental substances

(cont. from p. 15) Guardian Groups, her mission is to support humanity through its evolution with education, awareness, and by discussing the impacts of the energy shifts upon the planet, human beings, and human consciousness. She is an Ascension Guide, Planet Gridworker, Starseed Advocate, Humanitarian, Writer, and Educator for Disclosure and World Humanism."

to the emotional, mental, and "energetic quanta" or "life force" distribution. It is the main control mechanism and circuit board that governs the planet in every conceivable way. Clearly, these functions also greatly influence (or control) human beings to perceive themselves to what we believe to be a group consensus—to be the behavior/identity of a human being living on planet Earth. The planetary logos is the macrocosm function of the collective mind, and microcosm function of the individual mind. Planet Logos = Planetary Brain = Collective Race Mind = Human Mind = Individual Brain. All of these aspects of intelligence are an interactive part of the planetary logos.

The Planetary Logos, in turn, controls the messaging to the "planetary brain." These messages influence and control every living thing on the planet. The Archons (see plate 1) have modified this messaging such that the messages are being artificially programmed to create mind control, brain dysfunction, and blocking of nerve-synapse blockages. If we were informed and aware of these energy assaults against our consciousness, we could override them by creating an inner-spirit connection to be the priority incoming messaging system, and thus shield our auras.

Our Planetary Logos was invaded and corrupted by the Archons around the time of the Atlantean cataclysms, about 26,000 years ago. At that time, the human race was only about 15,000 years old, having been created to own this planet as a compromise between the Reptilians and the Elohim, a godlike human race from a distant star system. The ancient and powerful Atlanteans had been protecting us humans, but they were effectively destroyed by the cataclysms at that time, so we, as a very young race, were vulnerable to a takeover. Many of the Atlantean survivors fled to the Himalayas and other remote locations, where they founded wisdom schools. The Ascension Glossary describes the Archons this way:

These are extradimensional and interdimensional beings that have lost their consciousness connection to god source and are utilizing humans and other beings as their food source by siphoning life force like a parasite to live thousands of years. They do not have access to incarnate into human bodies so they covet human bodies and they want to take them over or use them in the future. They do not have emotions as humans have but are highly intelligent as they are working on mind principles higher than the human three layers of ego. They are similar to a Mad Scientist who manipulates and genetically modifies human beings, or as a farmer who is interested in gaining more resources out of his herd of cattle on the farm. They consider humans an investment in their energy resource portfolio. They can be best understood as a psychopathic or sociopathic personality or as [exhibiting an] identity profile with a lack of empathy, that has no feelings of remorse and no caring toward human beings. They regard human beings as inferior and stupid and many times [they] use forms of mockery [toward us] . . . for their own amusement.

These beings have been manipulating the human world of affairs for thousands and thousands of years, since the Atlantean cataclysms, for their own purposes. . . . They use many technological manipulation methods for mind control and negatively manipulate the future direction of the human race.

DRACOS, REPTILIANS, AND GRAYS

While the Archons dwell exclusively in the higher dimensions and are therefore invisible to human perception, various groups of Reptilians incorporate the Archontic energies and intentions, and they act as astral and physical extensions of the Archons.

Extraterrestrials (ETs) that are hybridized with Reptilian-based genetics operate in a strict hierarchical system of rank and defer to their superior groups. The Dracos or Draconians from Alpha Draconis are in command of Earth-based subterranean Reptilians, who respect their superiors in the belief that the "Dracs" hold "ownership" over Earth and human beings. Draco Reptilians (see plate 2) view themselves as the most intelligent species in the universe since they know that Earth humans are the result of a relatively recent biological seeding process from multiple planets.* The Alpha Draconis Dracos have a royal class, which appears to be lighter colored, having almost-white scales, with winged appendages. They are about two to three times the size of an average human and are much stronger. They are quite menacing and tyrannical, showing little mercy, even to members of their own race whom they think have defied their orders or shirked their responsibilities in the management of their "earthly resources." Earth-based Reptilians appear to be in command over biological entities known as the smaller "Grays." The Reptilians have developed high psionic abilities, which they use for mind controlling other species, and they do not have an emotional body or a soul body.

The known Reptilian races on Earth have made a variety of pacts with the higher ranks of human governmental and military organizations. These groups now compose a virtual shadow government. This has spawned "black" projects, such as secret space programs, military abductions (MILABs), and the creation of a military-industrial complex through which these groups can experiment with, and exploit, the alien-based technologies and craft to which they have been given access through their cooperation. The Dracs are an extremely militant, misogynistic, and warring species that are very involved in controlling the Power Elite and the financial, pharmaceutical, and banking institutions, and in promoting war and killing through increasing militarization, poverty consciousness, human enslavement and programming, political and religious violence, terrorism, and the harvesting of DNA from humans and other species that they have under their control.

THE ARCHONTIC DECEPTION STRATEGY

The Ascension Glossary describes the results of the Archontic invasion thus:

---

*We *Homo sapiens sapiens* were created by a federation of twelve humanlike species from other worlds who contributed their DNA to the Earth-human creation, which process was scientifically planned and managed by the Elohim. See my book, *Alien World Order: The Reptilian Plan to Divide and Conquer the Human Race.*

When our Planetary Logos was invaded and corrupted by the Archons, the planet and our race were impacted dramatically. It meant that we were no longer free to create and evolve as per the original blueprint of our intended creation, and we had no memory of what had happened to us. We were recycled through continual reincarnations through the Astral Plane with no memory of our past lives, who we really are, where we are going, or what our real relationship is to God and what humanity's "purpose" actually is. Over time most of us lost our feeling connection to our Soul Matrix and we became numb to the pain in order to survive in anti-human based structures. What has happened to our planet is not human, it is "alien" to the true nature of humanity. This is the Archontic Deception Strategy.

Since the Archons did respect our innate intelligence, because they know about the stellar spiritual origins of our souls, they knew that the strategic use of deception was critical to the takeover. It was necessary to secretly infiltrate our core societal organizational structures, such as our religious, medical, financial, and legal institutions, and to substitute artificial structures of their own design. This strategy, they knew, would also minimize their own efforts and force us to use our own energies and resources. It would allow them to shape the value systems that generate the belief systems they want to control. The Ascension Glossary says:

Through the engineering of a labyrinth of self-enforced enslavement policies based on fear and intimidation among the earth inhabitants, they would achieve the use of minimal "off planet" resources by piggy-backing on the earth-human resources. The people on earth would effectively enforce their own enslavement as well as enslave their own global human family by giving up their rights and their resources. This is very effective for a planetary invasion and take-over strategy because it generates minimal resistance or revolt by the inhabitants, who are unaware they are being invaded.

MIND CONTROL

The primary means of human enslavement by the Archons is mind control. According to the Ascension Glossary, when one has control over the mind, one has control over the directions and actions of the physical body and all of its parts and also over the ongoing mental effort to reclaim the soul energies. Consequently, whoever controls the mind also indirectly controls the soul.

Mind control is used to form socially acceptable belief systems and, at the same time, to create antihuman value systems, which are used to convince the masses to enslave themselves. This creates an oxymoronic death culture, which generates thoughts that are in contradiction to each other, like war and killing for peace. As long as the planet is at war with itself and humanity thinks we are at war with each other, we feed into the mind-control system of the Archons and Reptilians. God, religious violence, gender issues, financial and debt enslavement, consumptive modeling, and sexuality are the largest mind-controlled and manipulated belief systems promoted by the negative aliens and their human Power Elite, allowing them to continue their enslavement and vampirism of humanity and our planetary resources.

THE ARMAGEDDON SOFTWARE

Mind control is the main technique for imposing the false value systems that corrupted the original Planetary Logos and replaced the original planetary brain, thus substituting an artificial planetary brain. These alterations are imposed and enforced by the Power Elite, sometimes known as the Illuminati, who were originally empowered by the Archons. The Power Elite, at the highest level, operates through the three main pillars of society: the religious, financial, and academic institutions. These three pillars appear to be distinct, but they are really three different manifestations that have the same goal—the manipulation of humans to create the death culture and to enrich the controllers (i.e., the Power Elite). Once having control of the finances, the controllers are able to dominate the media and the press, to create wars and terrorism, and to shorten lives, thus advancing the death culture through the use of false medical practices and the poisoning of our physical bodies through tainted pharmaceuticals and vaccines, "chemtrails," and so forth.

The existing mind-control techniques are subtle and well disguised. They are implemented through the so-called Armageddon Software. This is a suite of mega-software applications designed by the Reptilians that has been programmed into the planetary brain. It relies on the planet-wide acceptance of patriarchal domination and the alien enslavement agenda. It uses holographic inserts of alien technology to project mind-control archetypes and instills self-enforced enslavement through such hallowed institutions as the Church of Rome and other forms of father-god religion, resulting in mind-control brainwashing based on the inculcation of religious fear. It operates by stirring up long-dead cellular memories of the cataclysms on Atlantis and Lemuria that have been erased from our conscious mind.

All of the Armageddon fears are a form of the planetary biowarfare mind-control programs to suppress and control human consciousness by propagating artificially generated false timelines, which are consciousness traps. They interfere with our continued spiritual growth and consciousness expansion. It is a part of the consciousness suppression of humanity in this Ascension cycle that forces reincarnation into the lower realms. This is a type of "soul recycling" for creating "worker bees" that are subservient to the on-planet and off-planet Archons. This acts as a power source for them that can be generated and then harvested from both the planetary body and human electromagnetic energy.

TARGETED POPULATION CONTROL

According to the Ascension Glossary:

To impact and manipulate mass human consciousness, all that is required is to create a complex signal through a frequency following response. When the brain locks onto an external signal coming from the environment it begins to mirror that signal. The signal can be a carrier wave of a Spectrum of Frequency designed to create feelings of distress or to trigger emotional pain. As a result, the brain chemistry alters and changes, generally plummeting the consciousness into a range of lower negative emotions and confused perceptions. Thus large populations can be sent frequencies that are designed to incite agitation, aggression, or anxiety in specific demographic areas.

This can be followed up with a news feed in the mainstream media into that same demographic area to incite fear or blame or to promote sensationalism using victimization language in order to single out certain marginalized groups for the intention of targeting them toward being perceived as the enemy, thereby inciting violence, rape, hostility, and criminal behaviors. It is possible to modulate signals on any electromagnetic carrier for transmitting a message into the brain to alter its chemistry, insert thought-forms, and instigate behaviors for shaping or grooming that person or persons to carry out some harmful or criminal actions.

Again, according to the Ascension Glossary:

Electromagnetic fields act as modulators of molecular-based information transfer; they can intercept and modify the processes of molecular interaction within a human body, in any kind of organism. As an example, the DNA can be altered, modified, or reversed when exposed to programmable broadcasts of electromagnetic fields, such as with ELFs. As a result electromagnetic fields can be used to control genetic switches or influence bio-chemical pathways and are capable of eliciting a range of effects inside a living organism, as well as in controlled environments or something taking place outside of living organisms. Exposures to electromagnetism affect organisms in both negative and positive ways, which are related to physiological processes, and the reaction is also connected to the genetic configuration and the consciousness level of the organism. The organism that has the lowest range of consciousness perception is generally the most impacted from the impulses coming from the Unconscious Mind. This is another example of how electromagnetic fields can be used for genetic engineering or modification purposes, by interfering with the Bio-Neurology and the body's natural biological system of information flow and transfer between DNA, RNA, and Proteins.

Artificial networks continually send out electromagnetic pulses of information through the mass media to keep people fixated on meaningless dramas, 3-D narratives, and negative emotions. The current role of mass media is to keep the CNS redirected toward a range of negative thoughts and to fixate or obsess on external physical stimulus or material things. In many forms of mass media and marketing, there are electronic-hacking attempts on the biological neural networks that signal messaging into the brain. In the media, whether through movies, internet, or any recreational medium, when focusing the person's attention on a series of light-and-sound images, these images transmit holographic information, sometimes transmitting frequency implants into the CNS and brain. The most popular form of mass media is the propaganda used by the Cabal for directing mind control, which is used to shape the person's brain activity and mental map. The content for mass consumption is produced and controlled to reflect light-and-sound holographic images that form what people believe is the nature of their reality.

When we have a better comprehension of how mind control is used in everyday mainstream media to produce divide-and-conquer belief systems, we can better discern the agenda and refuse to participate with it. The antidote to mind-control broadcasts is connecting with your inner spirit and developing your spiritual self every day with higher emotional qualities like empathy and compassion and genuinely caring about what happens to the human race and the planet.

3
The Rise to World Power

In the early twentieth century, when the Reptilians were ready for the final stage of their program to enslave the human race on this planet, their first priority was to select a country or racial group to work through—a group that could be relied on to carry out their very complex agenda of hybridization; artificial intelligence; poisoning of the air, food, and water; mind control, wars, and disasters; MILABs; and astral conditioning of the populace. They had to wait until the developments in science, technology, and industrialization had reached the point where their proto-human puppets, the Illuminati, were able to handle the complexities of their jobs. These Reptilian plans had been honed to perfection over thousands of years, during which time they had enslaved millions, perhaps billions, of the inhabitants of planets in twenty-one star systems in this galaxy (see my book *Alien World Order*). Choosing the Germans to attain these Reptilian goals was logical and tactical. More than any other racial group, the Germans were amazingly disciplined and able to achieve remarkable accomplishments by rapidly organizing huge industrial structures along hierarchical lines and ensuring that the reporting discipline from one level to another was efficient and highly regimented. This is the key to achieving results in large corporate, military, and governmental organizations. In this type of system, each departmental level has little or no knowledge of activity at other levels, and so, through this method, large numbers of employees can be made to produce products or carry out activities that are basically antisocial, inhuman, or even evil. It is this separation—keeping all groups on a strictly need-to-know basis by the management—that allows this to happen. The Reptilians knew this to be necessary because they didn't want to risk a rebellion in the ranks triggered by idealistic employees if their real objectives were uncovered. They intended to implement their takeover plans through large corporate entities, and secrecy was imperative. A capitalistic corporate-industrial structure was vital to their plans. They knew that democratic and socialistic political systems were antithetical to their program, and that is why they made sure to operate through antidemocratic and antisocialist authoritarian regimes.

The major problem with this structure is the lack of creativity. When workers are cowed into just "following orders," good ideas are repressed, and the consequences are a product or system that may be finished on time but lacks all the enhancements that would have been possible by incorporating the ideas and suggestions of subordinates all along the way. This tends to dilute the entire effort. But that is the price the elite are willing to pay to obtain the basic results. This is why it was possible for a kaiser and a führer to realize the accomplishment of their whims quickly, and so the Reptilian planners could depend on them to achieve their social, industrial, and military goals. Also, the German workers or soldiers didn't allow humane or ethical values to interfere with the process. To them, efficiency was everything, and human lives were just numbers. They just got the job done without regard for the human toll and with no regrets. In such an environment the leaders at the top (i.e., those who make policy), are all important, while the mid- and lower-level workers just take care of the simple, basically mindless, and repetitive tasks. These individuals are generally disposable and easily replaceable if they show any hesitation or signs of remorse. But eventually, the managers at the top don't want to bother with all the effort and the attention it takes to fool the workers into thinking they are doing something socially valuable. And so ultimately, they just resort to a form of slavery in which keeping track of salaries and recreation for their workers is no longer necessary. Then, doing away with all pretenses, they implement Gestapo-like tactics to control the organization and get their work done with outright slavery.

BLOOD AND IRON

The herculean job necessary to effect the emergence of a unified Germany as an armed scientific and industrial European power at the commencement of the twentieth century was basically due to the efforts and policies of one man: Prussian Prime Minister and later German Chancellor Otto von Bismarck. During the short period of his reign between 1862 and 1914, Germany was transformed from a collection of disputatious independent states to a comprehensive, politically unified, highly industrialized country under the dominance of Prussia. It began with the elevation of William I as king of Prussia in 1861, after the death of his brother, King Frederick William IV. William was dedicated to the unification of the German states. Believing that the best way to unify Germany was through war, he depended primarily on his war minister, Count von Roon. However, they were not able to build an effective military because of the liberal opposition in parliament. But then, in September 1862, William appointed Bismarck to the office of prime minister.

Bismarck was a force to be reckoned with. He essentially disregarded parliament and imposed new taxes dictatorially to pay for a new military. It was an illegal move, but as is often the case, strong, bold moves by one determined leader catch the vacillating opposition by surprise, and they cannot marshal enough unified forces to defeat his or her policies. In a speech to the parliament in 1862 to justify his actions, Bismarck uttered the famous phrase that has now echoed down through the years and that would come to characterize all such actions by future German dictators. He said, "The great questions of our time will be decided not by speeches and resolutions of majorities . . . but by blood and iron." This derogatory reference to "resolutions of majorities" was essentially a rejection of democracy and an endorsement of autocracy. And "blood and iron" could only mean one thing—warfare—which uses tons of iron and spills oceans of blood. This was a prophetic utterance by Bismarck because it was from that moment on that the new nation of Germany became a succession of dictatorships and began a worldwide reign of blood and iron for a period that lasted eighty-three years! This is overwhelming evidence that Bismarck was really an Illuminati, a Reptilian-human hybrid who was sent to implement the Reptilian agenda for the twentieth century. But, as with all things Reptilian, it was based on a lie because it really didn't answer "the great questions of our time" at all but rather provoked a new and horrifying direction for humanity that is still being played out.

THE SECOND INDUSTRIAL REVOLUTION

Bismarck was the first of a new generation of dictators, and he became the prototype of the autocratic German leaders who followed. He had multifaceted talents that allowed him to handle complicated political agendas with ease. He played other European political leaders against each other as though they were pawns on a chessboard and could achieve results that seemed impossible to others. He won three wars in quick succession, even though he himself was not really a military leader, each time enlarging Prussian territory and influence until Prussia became the new Germany. This allowed his autocratic successors, Kaiser Wilhelm II and Adolph Hitler, to inherit an enlarged and powerful nation. Perhaps most importantly, Bismarck's high intelligence permitted him to be at ease with the amazing industrial and technological advances that evolved during his reign, a time of changes that became known worldwide as the second industrial revolution.

Since Bismarck himself was an autocratic, conservative leader, he imbued the corporations that he fostered to be led the same way, especially Krupp AG and IG Farben. So the leaders of these corporations inherited the same vaunted greed, ambition, and indifference to human suffering as he displayed. He even set the stage for governmental anti-Semitism, which intensified later, even though the Jewish population in Prussia-Germany at that time was only 1 percent! An online announcement of a talk about his book *Bismarck: A Life,* by Jonathan Steinberg, held on May 26, 2011, by the Pears Institute for the Study of Antisemitism, based at Birkbeck, University of London, says, "Jonathan Steinberg will argue that Bismarck staged the first act of the 'tragedy of German Jewry.'" Steinberg argues that not only did anti-Semitism have deep roots in the aristocratic class from which Bismarck came (the Junkers), but also that Bismarck used it when it suited his politics. The first modern depression hit Germany in 1873, and Jews as prominent bankers took the blame. Bismarck abandoned his liberal allies and after 1878 set out to destroy them by crushing the Jews in their leadership. He allowed a wave of anti-Semitism to spread and watched as the Prussian parliament had its infamous "Jew Debate" in 1880—the first time the unified Germany declared that Jews were not real Germans.

REALPOLITIK

Bismarck's plan to develop Germany into a world power was ambitious and multifaceted, and certainly very difficult, if not impossible. It was highly pragmatic without any element of idealism. Playing heavily on Prussia's strong suits, he used what he had to good advantage and overcame the disadvantages by using war, and the threat of war, to get what he wanted. Germany was way behind Britain, France, and Belgium in terms of industrialization before 1850. But, according to Wikipedia, it had "a highly skilled labor force, a good educational system, a strong work ethic, good standards of living and a sound protectionist strategy." Bismarck parlayed these strengths into a very effective strategy so that by 1900, Germany was a world leader in industrialization, on a par with England and the United States! This, again according to Wikipedia, despite the fact that "until mid-century, the guilds, the landed aristocracy, the churches, and the government bureaucracies had so many rules and restrictions that entrepreneurship was held in low esteem, and given little opportunity to develop."

It really was a remarkable achievement and testifies to Bismarck's bold and unique mental powers, a characteristic that we now know to be identified with the Reptilians. It helped that Bismarck was not really attached to any particular ideology, which gave him perfect flexibility, and that he was a virtual dictator. Thus he was able to use what became known as Realpolitik, that is, when it comes to world power, "any means to an end" or "the ends justify the means." It can also be called "power politics" because power on the international stage is the only consideration. It can sometimes be described as "peace through strength." Realpolitik is an old and popular technique that has been practiced by venerated world leaders since ancient times. Perhaps most famous were Niccolo Machiavelli, the Italian political philosopher who wrote *The Prince,* Frederick the Great of Prussia, Carl von Clausewitz, author of *On War,* and of course, Napoleon Bonaparte. Adolf Hitler may not have been aware of his philosophical debt to these men, but he proved to be an adept practitioner of Realpolitik, grabbing Czechoslovakia and Austria without firing a shot. It's not to say that these men were necessarily unprincipled, but rather that they understood well, and endorsed, the real underpinnings of world power.

A WELFARE STATE

Through his political machinations, Bismarck created a climate in which industry could thrive, and consequently, huge German conglomerates evolved and rapidly caught up with those in the West. Bismarck helped them along by instituting welfare programs for German industrial workers as early as the 1880s. He introduced old age programs, accident insurance, medical care insurance, and unemployment insurance, thus making Germany a virtual welfare state. Keeping the workers happy also kept the owners happy and allowed Germany to rocket to the top of the world industrial hierarchy. In particular, the German chemical, coal mining, steel, railroads, and agricultural combines became world class, primarily through the formation of cartels. The iron and steel companies bought the coal mines, which formed integrated production facilities, because steel manufacture requires large admixtures of coke. These mixed firms, so-called Konzerns, multiplied rapidly, so that coal output went from 2 million tons in 1850 to 130 million tons in 1940, thus setting the stage for the massive Krupp works and the fearsome Nazi weaponry of World War II.

The railroads were critical to German unification. Through the 1830s, each of the thirty-seven states had its own railroad systems, but by the 1840s, trunk lines connected the individual networks. And then, by the time of the creation of the German Empire in 1871, the national railroad system was in place and growing and approaching equality with the British system. This spurred the growth and nationalization, especially the urbanization, of the steel industry, which then developed rapidly and spread to university centers of research and development. As a result of this linkage between research and the manufacturing laboratories, Germany developed a rich and sophisticated chemical industry and quickly became a leader in chemicals. The founding of the Bayer Corporation and the BASF Laboratories in the 1880s (see plate 3) catapulted Germany to dominance in world chemicals so that by the outbreak of World War I in 1914, Germany had achieved 90 percent of the entire share of international volumes of trade in chemical products!

Fig. 3.1. Farben headquarters

As we will see, this early monopolization of the chemical industry had important ramifications for World War II, when in 1925, these two huge corporations joined four others to form the gigantic IG Farben Cartel.

FASCISM BY CARTELIZATION

But it was in banking that the German cartels had the most pronounced effects. By pooling money for investment and avoiding all the destructive effects of competition, the German banks and investment houses were able to pinpoint the financing of important industries. And this focus was, in turn, subject to the pressures of governmental policies. Consequently, the banks responded to the dictates of Bismarck for financing his wars. Jointly, they directed large pools of funds to industries that Bismarck deemed important to his political agenda. Freed of the waste of time and money brought about by competition, Germany could enjoy the efficiencies of socialism without the negative aspects. One of the main benefits of socialism is that the government owns the means of production, instead of individuals or corporations. That allows the people to have a major voice in government financial and production policies, and theoretically to distribute the profits. Since in this case, the cartels have wider ownership, the system becomes almost socialistic. This *almost* works in a democracy, but not in an autocracy such as Germany during both World Wars. The negative aspects of which I spoke means that all incentives to individuals for success go away when they are supported by the government. Under fascism, all of the cronies of the leader get rich because he diverts all the business to his friends' corporations, but everyone else becomes cannon fodder, as in Nazi Germany and in present-day Russia. Thus the German banking cartels created cooperative financing of major industries and entered into a sort of partnership with the autocratic leaders, which is really the essence of fascism. So German fascism really began in the late nineteenth century and then flowered under Hitler in the twentieth century when the banks and war producers worked in open partnership.

Bismarck did his job well by laying the groundwork for dictator number two, Kaiser Wilhelm II. Bismarck's three successful wars had enriched the coffers of the new German Empire and had given it a new geography in which to develop its industrial might and military preparations and from which to seek a greater enlargement of territory. But the kaiser had a much more ambitious agenda in mind for the future of Europe. For the kaiser, Bismarck had not been aggressive enough, and after only two years of contention between the two men, Bismarck, now, in his seventies, too old and tired to confront the new forceful and belligerent twenty-nine-year-old German leader, decided to call it quits in 1890. After all, Bismarck was just a commoner, while the kaiser had inherited the royal Reptilian-human hybrid bloodline of Queen Victoria. The Reptilian High Command was already planning ahead to Adolf Hitler, and they needed the kaiser to set the stage.

Fig. 3.2. Kaiser Wilhelm II

4

The German Population Transformation

David Icke pointed out in The Biggest Secret *that the actual rulers of this planet are Reptilians who reside in the lower fourth dimension and who work through their reptilian-human hybrids that have attained positions of power on Earth. These reptilian-human hybrids are the driving force behind most of the systemic cruelty and wickedness on Earth.*

JAMES BARTLEY

Side by side with the swift emergence of Germany as an empire in 1871, and as a world industrial power in 1900, was the transformation of the German populace. They morphed from a peace-loving, relatively liberal agrarian society to a cosmopolitan, cynical, and sophisticated citified people with a decided imperialistic and prideful orientation. How did this happen over such a short period, from 1871 to 1900?

The ability of the Archons to program the consciousness of targeted large groups of individuals made it possible for them to divide and conquer the human race by setting the citizens of one nation against those of another, or for that matter, to the rest of the human race, as explained

34

in chapter 1. That appears to be precisely what happened at the beginning of the twentieth century. The Germanic race was selected by the Archons to become a "chosen people," precisely as were the Hebrews two thousand years earlier.

Since this amazing event was accomplished at an interdimensional level, the German citizenry had no conscious knowledge of what had transpired. They simply began to believe that they were a special people chosen by God, or the gods, to rule over the other peoples of the Earth because they were naturally mentally and spiritually superior, and therefore God wanted them to step up to their divine responsibility. And if this led to mass bloodshed, so be it, precisely as was the case with the Hebrews in the Old Testament, who were instructed by Jehovah "to leave not a soul alive." Since these individual beliefs percolated up from the lower realms of the Fourth Dimension, how could the targeted groups, at the conscious level, ever be aware of their origins at the subconscious level? Hitler tapped into this fiction by telling the German populace that they were superior, and the other races were bestial and like animals. That is how he convinced them to invade Russia and to slaughter civilians.

So that is how the Archons were able to prepare the early twentieth-century generation of the German population (and the Japanese, too) for a century of aggression and war. Through abduction and hybridization, the German and Japanese children were genetically created to have a higher percentage of Reptilian blood, perhaps as much as 50 percent. Presumably, the Archons then programmed the males in this category, who were to become the foot soldiers, with lower intelligence and emotionality, making it easier for them to adopt brutality and insensitivity toward those they regarded as inferior. Also, they were programmed with a built-in misogyny—a contempt for women and all feminine values. The females, correspondingly, were programmed to support these attitudes in their leaders and their male partners. As discussed in the previous chapter, the Archons themselves had absolutely no remorse for heaping misfortune on human beings and using them for horrible experiences. Thus the proto-human hybrids were ready to wreak havoc and cruelty on the human race, and they did so, on both military and civilian targets, without distinction, as will be discussed in the next chapter.

ASTRAL DREAMSCAPE MANIPULATION

Probably the most pervasive method for programming individuals to acquire certain mental and emotional characteristics is the invasion of the astral body of the targeted individuals while asleep. Once these people have been prepared for astral influence by genetic selection, abduction, and hybridization, they are then marked for nighttime attention. The most experienced and knowledgeable researcher, by far, on this subject is James Bartley.

Bartley is a longtime occult researcher who specializes in the Reptilian influence. In his own words, "My name is James Bartley and I am a colleague of Eve Lorgen. I am an abductee. I am a student of military history and have studied the occult connection with the UFO phenomenon. We humans reside in what is essentially a reptilian sphere of influence. The symbology of the reptilian overlordship is all around us. Phallic worship and the marginalization of the feminine principle have reduced the human race to what it is today, a *thundering herd of bewildered sheep*."

In his online article "Astral Dreamscape Manipulation," Bartley says, "Astral Dreamscape Manipulation is a very pervasive form of behavior modification that most abductees experience at one time or another. Sadly, most abductees are oblivious to the fact that this is an aspect of behavior modification that is routinely practiced by the reptilians upon certain categories of abductees."

He explains further, "The reptilians hold the tactical 'High Ground' in the astral dreamscape by dint of the fact that most humans are not lucid dreamers and the reptilians are 'at home' in the astral dreamscape. Besides being para-physical entities and mesmerizers par excellence, reptilians can shape and influence a dreamscape experience to suit their devious and sordid ends. Moreover the reptilians can further diminish what little lucidity and awareness humans may have in the dreamscape. The reptilians are intimately familiar with the way the Human Mind works and in particular how to create certain imagery or set the mood of a 'dream.'"

Most humans, no matter how practiced in psychic and/or paranormal capabilities they may be, are no match for the mental powers of these Reptilian "psychic soldiers." Even experienced human astral travelers or remote viewers cannot comprehend and unmask the trickery of the Reptilian techniques. In this regard, Bartley says, "The reptilians and their minions are masters of creating illusions, assuming disguises, and dimming the awareness of human beings in or out of the astral dreamscape. In the dreamscape the reptilians can heighten the anxiety level of the abductee or promote mental sluggishness just as easily as if they were spinning the dial on an FM radio."

PROMOTING VIOLENCE

The Reptilian ability to plant imagery in the minds of the sleeping humans can be used just to harden the sensitivities to extreme and horrible wartime scenarios. Bartley says, "Abductees can be made to eat what appears to be raw meat, bloody 'pancakes,' or even human body parts such as hands in the astral dreamscape. Abductees have been known to suffer extreme nausea lasting for weeks or months after being subjected to this kind of manipulation. I cannot stress enough the importance of never eating or drinking anything in the astral dreamscape"—that is, if you have conscious awareness of that or enough control to do that.

Using these techniques, the Reptilians can turn normally peace-loving males into raging mass murderers to condition them for war. Bartley says:

Violent and sociopathic behaviors can also be promoted through astral dreamscape manipulation. Children, teenagers, and adults can be shown images of blood and gore in the astral dreamscape and can even be compelled to participate in violent scenarios in which the abductee is made to either watch or take part in horrific acts of violence. . . . Regarding violence as a conditioned response, I know personally an adult male who was made to kill his wife and children again and again in the astral dreamscape. The killings would always be done in a gory vicious fashion. His waking hours were no relief either as "voices in his head" urged him to act on the "fantasies" he'd been having and murder his entire family. He told me that he could understand how someone could be made to kill after they had been subjected to this type of treatment for a while.

Violent tendencies within males can be fostered by [another] . . . type of manipulation. It is especially useful if the male is the partner of a female abductee who the reptilians want to keep in a state of physical and sexual degradation. The reptilians will use Tarzan as their proxy handler. Often times, if Tarzan is hosted himself or if he is being plied with deviant erotic mental imagery, he will begin to manifest deviant sexual desires including acting out fantasies of bondage and discipline upon his hapless girlfriend or wife. Vulgarity, sexual perversion, and the need to control others are hallmarks of the reptilian influence upon human beings.

THE LOVE BITE

Violent tendencies can also be promoted within male abductees undergoing the "alien love bite." Barbara Bartholic and Eve Lorgen have made in-depth studies of this form of alien manipulation. A French journalist who interviewed Bartholic said, "Barbara is the greatest alien abduction researcher in the world, bar none." In an interview in 1997, Eve Lorgen said of herself, ". . . I have been running an abductee support group in San Diego County for several years (since 1991). I have a master's degree in Counseling Psychology, experience in hypnosis, and have been an abductee since childhood." Jointly, Bartholic and Lorgen, who are also associates of James Bartley, said, "During the latter stages of the love-bite manipulation, a male abductee can become enraged at the female he has become obsessed with. The aliens will send images into the mind of the male abductee of his targeted love-bite partner having sexual intercourse with another man. It is as if a videotape is playing in the mind of the male abductee, which is designed to drive him crazy with rage."

MILABS AND KAPOS

Out of all the many categories of Reptilian abductees who are trained consciously or not for various jobs required to maintain the Reptilian "occupation," there is one type that is highly valued over all the others—someone who can be trained to become a reliable and useful asset to carry out specific types of assignments under the control of so-called Deep Black military professionals who are themselves experienced Reptilian hybrids, or "hubrids." This technique of training slaves to become managers of other slaves is a time-honored Reptilian system to conserve their own resources and energies for only the most critical operations, while those in the rank and file of the slave population are awarded some types of minor rewards or advantages if they can be used to train and supervise other low-level slaves.

This system was revealed at its most effective in the Nazi concentration camps wherein the camp administrators selected prisoners, called *kapos,* to manage the other prisoners. The employment of this system as early as 1940, long before the Reptilians had made slaves out of the concentration camp inmates, tells us that the Reptilians must view the entire human race essentially as a slave population!

According to Wikipedia:

A kapo or prisoner functionary . . . was a prisoner in a Nazi concentration camp who was assigned by the SS guards to supervise forced labor or carry out administrative tasks. Also called "prisoner self-administration," the prisoner functionary system minimized costs by allowing camps to function with fewer SS personnel. The system was designed to turn victim against victim, as the prisoner functionaries were pitted against their fellow prisoners in order to maintain the favor of their SS overseers. If they were derelict they would be returned to the status of ordinary prisoner and be subject to other kapos. Many prisoner functionaries were recruited from the ranks of violent criminal gangs rather than from the more numerous political, religious, and racial prisoners; such criminal convicts were known for their brutality toward other prisoners. This brutality was tolerated by the SS and was an integral part of the camp system.

The use of this system by the Nazis is clear evidence that the entire Nazi population, but especially the SS, was simply a front for the Reptilians, who we now know were in league with Hitler. It cannot be a coincidence that the Nazis adopted this Reptilian system of slave control in the concentration camps if they hadn't learned it from their Reptilian overlords.

This technique has been a hallmark of Reptilian management of an enslaved planet that they have used throughout their empire of twenty-one conquered star systems. Its adoption by the Nazis is clear evidence that the Nazi regime was influenced by the Reptilians. It has been used throughout human history wherever the Reptilians remained in secret underground control of the surface population. Its virtue is simple: let the conquered populations enslave themselves by using human lieu-tenants who have been hybridized, which makes them supremely cor-ruptible and uncaring about their fellow humans. Where the Reptilian bloodline prevails, there is almost no human compassion or love. It is not in their DNA. This frees up the scarce Reptilian assets to handle only the most critical supervisory functions.

Putting this system in operation is a multistage operation. First, they seek out the best candidates for hybridization. They prefer militar-ily trained and disciplined men for this first rank. They are abducted and used to contribute their human DNA to the hybrid DNA. The resulting hybrid progeny really have little or no concern for the human race, just as their progenitors, the Reptilians themselves, have nothing but contempt for humans. They are completely cold-blooded managers who can play cards while humans are being tortured. The Reptilians then incorporate these hybrid men into human military organizations, where they frequently attain high rank. These are the Deep Black controllers. Their job in stage 2 of the operation is to abduct other humans and program them through hypnosis to carry out specific functions among the human population. In recent times, since the 1950s, these types of individuals, who are managed by the Deep Black controllers, are called Milabs, short for "military abductees" because almost all the Deep Black controllers are in the military.

Wherever in human history there has been a large slave population, such as in ancient Egypt and Rome, it can be deduced that the entire population is under firm Reptilian control. That was the case in ancient Egypt under the pharaohs when all the Hebrews were enslaved, and that was why it was so critical for Jehovah to separate them out of the general population by the Exodus and give them their own land in order for them to develop advanced spirituality.

USING MILABS

Bartley says, "In all likelihood Milabs have some kind of genetic marker that identifies them as legitimate alien abductees. This notion is buttressed by the fact that alien abductees who have served in the armed forces have described mind control, medical experimentation, and other coercive measures perpetrated upon them during their stints in the military. They have also described being utilized in covert operations while in a mind-controlled state. Some of them have been shown advanced technology and have witnessed non-human life forms in underground and above ground installations."

The training of milabs is intense and comprehensive. They are trained for a wide variety of jobs, most of which appear to be for conventional warfare roles in the physical plane (i.e., the Third Dimension). In other words, these men and women are primarily conditioned to become "supersoldiers" in the army, navy, and air force, in actual combat roles. This tells us that the Milabs are being created for jobs that require a military demeanor and advanced military skills, unlike the individuals discussed above, who are simply being conditioned in the astral dreamscape to accustom civilians to Reptilian control and who may be used for a wide variety of roles when the Reptilians reveal themselves openly as our slave masters. Those people likely will become the kapos at that time, and the Milabs will become the soldiers. Both techniques were used on the German and Japanese populations in the early twentieth century.

HOSTILE INTERROGATIONS OF FEMALE MILABS

According to Bartley:

Milabs are sometimes brought to a military facility, the locations of which are oftentimes underground, and are subjected to hostile interrogations and outright torture. The "interrogations" are really not interrogations at all. Usually the milab, very often a female milab, is asked the same question over and over. It is a question that the milab cannot answer because she doesn't know the answer. The female milab may be injected with a drug or she may have a drug introduced into her system by intravenous drip. The real purpose behind the interrogation is to provide her captors with an excuse to torture her. She may be made to sit on a chair with her arms tied to the back of the chair and her ankles tied to the legs of the chair. The interrogators may use hand-held devices that give her a powerful electric shock. They may shock her quite close to her heart. After they strip her of her clothing they may even shove the device up her vagina and shock her from within her body. The female milab may also be suspended from the ceiling, hanging either by her arms or her feet. During this entire ordeal she will receive numerous slaps, punches, and kicks from her captors.

The military feel that the female milab's psi abilities will be at their peak only after she has endured this kind of torture. I am somewhat dubious of this demented "reasoning." From the short-term standpoint the female milabs thus abused may indeed have higher than normal psi abilities, but in the long term the female milabs may be more uncooperative. The female milabs I have spoken to who have endured such experiences express nothing but contempt and hatred for their controllers, whereas in the past they may have been more cooperative. There are many female milabs who would gladly volunteer and work for the milab controllers in order to avoid the torture I've just described. Oftentimes the female milab being tortured is told that her children or other family members may be killed or similarly tortured if she refuses to answer the questions given to her. Sometimes the military controllers will abduct and torture close family members of the female milab to let her know that they are serious and not to be trifled with. You can imagine how the female milab feels after one of her children reports having a bad dream of being beaten and tortured by military personnel. Especially in light of what had happened to her.

The real purpose behind all this sadistic torture, as demented as it sounds, is to "splinter the splinters" i.e. fragment the female milab's already dissociated and fragmented mind. This allows the military controllers to do the following: store information in a particular compartment in her mind; extract information from a particular compartment in her mind; utilize her in astral and remote viewing ops at a deeper psychic level; and ensure the milab forgets the whole traumatic experience.

By abusing and torturing female milabs in this fashion, the military accomplishes two inter-related goals: First, the female milab is terrified beyond belief and her psyche is fragmented even more than it was in the past thus enabling her controllers to utilize her psychic abilities when they are presumably at their peak. Second, the systematic abuse meted out to the female milabs provides "training" for military personnel and conditions them to behave in this fashion without any compunctions or guilt whatsoever. Some military men are not cut out for this kind of work and may be removed from this program if they cannot torture or rape these women.

It is noteworthy that the male milabs are not treated with such gleeful sadism as the females. They are simply "toughened up" and conditioned not to feel any sympathy or remorse for the way the females, or the civilian population in general, even children, are treated. In fact, male milabs frequently develop a sort of camaraderie with their tormentors, in much the same way as freshmen at military schools or basic trainees in the military ultimately develop gratitude toward their trainers for transforming them into hardened monsters. This male favoritism clearly reveals the misogyny of the Reptilians, who are known to despise females. This may be the result of the humiliation they were forced to endure on their native planets in Draco and Orion when the females tamed the males and deliberately shortened their lives through drugs. That was the age of the legendary Queens of Orion. So now, in their off-planet colonies, they can take their revenge for this gender-humbling history by keeping the females "in their place."

THE NEW GENERATION

The generation of people born in Germany between 1870 and 1910 was very different from preceding generations and deserves a new appellation, just as the different generations in America have been assigned names consistent with their apparent characteristics. When we now speak about baby boomers, Gen Xers, or millennials, we know immediately the sort of individuals that belong in those groups because they do, generally speaking, share certain obvious traits regardless of gender or racial or ethnic derivation. Being born at a certain time in history in a place with the same cultural environment confers a certain similarity of temperament. These designations seem to apply only to Americans because they have been born into a social nexus that is purely American. So it was the same for the Germans born into that era in Germany, even if we have never before categorized Germans by generation, because the traits for that particular group are so starkly identifiable.

These individuals seem to have been realistic and world-weary from birth. They displayed what is known as *weltschmerz,* which is defined as "world pain." Very different from the generation that preceded them, they preferred watching military parades to dancing in the park, as people did in the Gay Nineties. They were anything but romantic, preferring utter realism to any sort of fanciful imaginings. Their inborn "world weariness" manifested as a certain type of coldness and hardness that allowed them to countenance brutal and even horrible events without a reaction. They could just yawn and turn away. They seemed to lack empathy and compassion for their fellow humans. And this is precisely the sort of temperament that was required for a century of "blood and iron." It was, in fact, they who created it. This generation in Germany was the calculated result of an influx of hybrids with a much higher percentage of Reptilian blood than previously. This was by Reptilian design, since they can control that process by the genetics used in mass abductions. We know, by now, that the Reptilians are master geneticists. When astral dreamscape influence and negative Archontic programming were added into the mix, they had the perfect recipe for the new humans. Also, if this generation consisted of a larger than usual percentage of alien-human hybrids, then that, in itself, could explain the characteristics of this generation because hybrid bodies cannot accommodate human souls. And if these hybrids were placed in positions of financial and political power, then that would definitely account for the unique generational character.

These individuals were not given to sentimentality or dismay when witnessing human cruelty or suffering because they were really only partly human themselves. Also, clearly, they had a disposition toward enslavement of others, whenever possible, since they were contemptuous toward those weaker than themselves, whom they believed should be used to do all the hard work of life, while they supervised. And so it is not surprising that this generation could commit the Herero Genocide (see chapter 6) or could be attracted to becoming Nazis or could easily adapt to using slave labor on other planets. For convenience, they could all be referred to as Nazis, but this term refers only to those who adopted that particular political philosophy and orientation during a few decades in the mid-twentieth century. The best descriptive and all-inclusive term for this German generation, the one that has now clearly revealed itself, would be *nonhuman*. But this is misleading. So, it would be better to continue to use *proto-human*.

The arrival of the proto-human German generation coincided with the advent of the kaiser in 1888. This, of course, was not accidental. It was planned by the Archons many years in advance. Bismarck had laid the foundation of the new unified Germany. This became the German Empire in 1871, probably because the kaiser wanted to think of himself as an emperor when he ascended to the throne. The kaiser was a poster boy for the proto-human generation. He displayed every characteristic previously mentioned and one more that was not yet clearly evident in the general population—total dishonesty.

PART 2

OPPRESSION, COLONIZATION, REVOLT, AND GENOCIDE

5

The Colonial Era

By the 1880s, the basic transformation of the first generation of the German population of the new century had been completed. This newest generation had been programmed from the astral plane to be unfeeling and cruel. They would be young adults (i.e., twenty to thirty-five years old) by 1900, which would be at the height of the colonial era. These men carried out their inner directions for control over the native populations coldly and brutally. Then this generation would be just the right age to be in the officer class (i.e., thirty-five to fifty years old) by World War I, when those same traits, on a higher level, would also be useful. So in addition to having been programmed at the astral level, they would also have the advantage of fifteen years of colonial experience, military and otherwise, to become effective officers in the war and to be positioned to treat their enemies as they had the natives. As will be seen in the next chapter, they would be completely ruthless in their treatment of civilians before World War I.

These men would then either be dead or aging veterans when World War II began in 1939. That was why it was necessary to create an entirely new fighting force for the Second World War. And those men had to be even more hardened to cruelty in order to stomach the brutalities of the new war, especially the slaughter and enslavement of the conquered civilians and workers and the horrors of the concentration camps. Essentially, without that critical colonial experience, they had to be more robotic, to be trained to just obey orders and feel no sympathies or remorse toward their victims, to leave the strategies and cruelties up to those connected to the occult organizations surrounding Hitler, especially Heinrich Himmler, the head of the Nazis' feared paramilitary organization, the Schutzstaffel (the SS). So those necessities support the thesis advanced in my previous books, that Hitler's Reptilian allies cloned an entirely new million-man army for World War II. But, as will be explained later, these soldiers were not really clones: they were cyborgs—part human and part machine—trained only to obey orders. These Wehrmacht (the widely used German word for the German army during WWII) cyborgs then became the cannon fodder needed for the attack against Russia on the eastern front, where they knew the casualties would be enormous. But also, because they were essentially robots and had no sympathies for humans, they would never hesitate to commit genocide when commanded, as they did in Russia. So they were, in effect, disposable robotic monsters.

THE BERLIN CONFERENCE

By 1884, the amazing emergence of Germany as a world industrial power in such a short time caught the rest of the Western world, including the United States, by surprise. As previously discussed, this was the result of the Bismarck "miracle." In that year, Portugal called for a world conference to address the partition of Africa. Nobody expected Germany to participate in such a conference because it was still regarded as a newcomer on the world power scene and had only a minor role in the colonization of Africa. Germany, knowing this, realized that it was necessary to assure the other powers of their noble intentions regarding the treatment of the natives.

Consequently, they were perfectly willing to join in the solemn pledge to (a) preserve the aboriginal races of Africa, (b) watch over their interests, and (c) cultivate their moral and material advancement and development. In July 1890, Germany went even further to convince the other nations of its civilized goals for Africa. They attended the Anti-Slavery Conference in Brussels, wherein they were placed on record by a solemn pledge and resolution that it was "the emphatic desire of the conferring Powers effectively to protect the native races of Africa from oppression and slavery." It was this pledge that permitted them to be welcomed into the "colonial club" and that opened up a treasure trove of territory for annexation to their land-locked nation. About this, the *British Blue Book* of 1918 says, "It is not to be wondered at, therefore, knowing what Germany's declared and avowed native policy was, that the statesmen and people of Great Britain had no hesitation in welcoming that Power into the arena of world colonization as a co-partner in the great work of civilizing and uplifting the heathen races of the earth. It was apparently in this spirit, and on those pledged assurances at Berlin and Brussels, that Great Britain allowed Germany to annex 322,450 square miles of territory in Southwest Africa, and by a stroke of the pen placed the Ovambos, Hereros, Damaras, Hottentots, Bastards, and Bushmen of that vast land under the guardianship and control of the German Emperor." As we will see, these promises were as empty as the consciences from which they had sprung, and they were soon abandoned.

The promises made at the Anti-Slavery Conference were made after the kaiser had come to power in 1888, so it can reasonably be inferred that it was he who made these commitments, and not Chancellor Bismarck, who had retired by then. What is astounding here is the gross hypocrisy of the kaiser when it is realized to what astonishing degree these promises were violated. It was he himself who backed Army Lieutenant-General Lothar von Trotha and approved the Herero genocidal slaughter and slavery (see chapter 6).

It was France and Belgium that had the most to gain and the most to lose in that conference. Belgium dominated the colonization of Central Africa, and France was in clear control of North and

West Africa. And yet, it was Bismarck who was chosen to convene and organize the conference because the newly unified Germany had such universal recognition as a growing manufacturing, mercantile, and military presence in both Europe and Africa. Because Bismarck was the organizer, it was Berlin that was chosen to host the meeting, and thus this became known as the Berlin Conference of 1884–1885. This convocation played the central role in what became known as the new imperialism, as the European powers flexed their muscles and began looking for new acquisitions to bolster their economic and territorial ambitions, and it was primitive Africa, rich in land and valuable natural resources but posing no military threat, that beckoned.

There was never any question about military opposition from the natives because Africa was still such a backward continent and the scattered tribes had many confusing languages and dialects and no military organization. So the European powers tried to grab what they could, but they had to parcel out spheres of influence to avoid conflict among themselves. That was the purpose of the conference. So it is no surprise to learn that, according to Wikipedia, "One of the goals of the conference was to reach agreements over trade, navigation, and boundaries of Central Africa. However, of all of the 15 nations in attendance . . . none of the countries represented were African." During this period, British influence in Africa was waning, while that of Germany and the United States was growing. But England was still very much a factor worldwide in the new imperialism. With its globe-spanning and unmatched fleet, England looked farther eastward to Asia to plant its flag and decided to bypass Africa and to instead absorb India into its sphere of influence to gain control of the lucrative spice trade. But they did also make some claims in East Africa, which ultimately became Bechuanaland. The conference became known as "the Scramble for Africa." Ultimately, England, France, Belgium, Germany, and Portugal mapped out their territorial claims and agreed on free trade all over the continent.

THE SULTAN RELENTS

The first German colony in Africa was established by a small company led by adventurer Karl Peters on the East African coast opposite the island of Zanzibar, based on treaties that Peters had negotiated with local chieftains for a vast tract of land comprising about sixty thousand square miles. On March 3, 1885, Bismarck granted an imperial charter to Peters for these colonies. Thus this became a German protectorate. Peters quickly moved to expand the colony north and south along the coast. The sultan of Zanzibar protested that he owned all that land. Bismarck then reluctantly sent five warships to support the protectorate, with guns trained on the sultan's palace. The sultan relented, and thus the Germans had their first legal colony in Africa, called German East Africa. This territory now comprises the modern nations of Tanzania, Burundi, and Rwanda. Peters used small local armed mercenary contingents for security, consisting mainly of lower-ranked military men. His men developed a reputation for brutality, including the hanging and flogging of the natives. So already the programmed Archon/Reptilian cruelty began to emerge. According to Wikipedia, "Travelers and newspaper reporters brought back stories of black and brown natives serving German managers and settlers [as slaves]. There were also suspicions and reports of colonial malfeasance, corruption, and brutality in some protectorates, and Lutheran and Roman Catholic missionaries dispatched disturbing reports to their mission headquarters in Germany. But the colonial economy was thriving . . . and roads, railways, shipping, and telegraph communications were up to the minute." Much of this rapid development was facilitated by harshly treated native labor, amounting to semi-enslavement. Increasingly, reports of German oppression began to filter back to the European newspapers. According to the *New World Encyclopedia,* "Rebellions, when they took place, were brutally crushed."

THE HEREROS AND NAMAS

The Herero natives were peaceful cattle traders living in the vast territory in Southwest Africa on the Atlantic coast that had been annexed to Germany by Great Britain at the Anti-Slavery Conference and had become a German protectorate. The Hereros were in conflict with another tribe and requested assistance from the Germans to help them. On October 21, 1895, the Herero chief, Maharero, signed a protection treaty with Germany's colonial governor, Heinrich Göring, who was the father of Hermann Göring, later to emerge as Hitler's commander of the German air force, the Luftwaffe. But this was strictly a mutual-assistance pact, and the Hereros did not cede any land to Germany. The treaty lapsed for two years starting in 1888, but then resumed in 1890. By this time Bismarck had stepped down and his duties as head of state had been taken over by Kaiser Wilhelm II in 1888. Wilhelm quickly became known to be more racially insensitive and severe in his treatment of the African natives. This attitude fostered German colonial crimes against the natives.

In 1890, Maharero's son Samuel succeeded his father as chief and signed over a large parcel of land to the Germans in return for their endorsement of his elevation to becoming the primary native representative in dealing with the Germans. But nothing improved. According to Wikipedia, "Under German colonial rule, natives were routinely used as slave laborers, and their lands were frequently confiscated and given to colonists, who were encouraged to settle on land taken from the natives; that land was stocked with cattle stolen from the Hereros and Namas, causing a great deal of resentment. Over the next decade, the land and the cattle that were essential to Herero and Nama lifestyles passed into the hands of German settlers arriving in Southwest Africa." Herero women and girls were reportedly frequently raped by German colonists, crimes that were greeted by a "wink and a nod" in Berlin. In 1894, Theodore Leutwein, a lawyer from Berlin in the same socio-economic class as the kaiser, was appointed governor of the protectorate, supported by a German paramilitary contingent to maintain order and ethnic peace. But the real purpose of this troop was to protect the colonists from native incursions.

This contingent, called the Schutzgruppe, initially consisted of about 160 men, mostly white settlers and mercenaries, organized into three platoons, which included two machine-gun teams, along with native irregulars. By the outbreak of World War I in 1914, about 300 European soldiers and 2,500 natives had been added. The Schutzgruppe in Africa was originally under the command of Bismarck and then the emperor, but was never part of the Imperial German Army. It remained under the Colonial Office.

THE REVOLT

By 1903, the Hereros and Namas had ceded over 25 percent of their land, originally about fifty thousand square miles, to German colonists. Most of this was just taken over by the colonists, backed by the Schutzgruppe. A railroad line from the coast to the inland territory was underway and would have opened the colony to a tidal wave of new German settlers when completed. These were the two main reasons, on top of the previous abuses by the Germans, for the Herero and Nama Revolt of 1903. Additionally, the natives were in the habit of borrowing money from the colonists at exorbitant interest rates. When Governor Leutwein announced a new policy of forgiving debts not paid in a year, the colonists started to grab cattle and anything else they could get their hands on as repayment. According to the *British Blue Book,* "The famous Credit Ordinance was promulgated in the middle of that year. Traders were (against Leutwein's direct advice) given one year in which to collect outstandings, which would be proscribed thereafter, and they fell upon the Herero cattle like a pack of ravenous wolves." This added fuel to the existing fire of native resentment. And if that wasn't enough, the Hereros learned of a plan to divide their country in half when the railroad was completed and to put the natives on reservations like the Native Americans in the American Southwest. That did the trick. In early 1904, the natives organized militarily and launched a carefully planned surprise attack. They killed about 150 colonists, including three women.

ANNIHILATION BY GRADUAL DESTRUCTION

Encouraged by their initial victories, led by Chief Samuel Maharero, the Hereros surrounded the small city of Okahandja and cut communication links to the colonial capital, thus cutting off German reinforcements. Maharero then issued a manifesto forbidding his troops to kill any Englishmen, Boers (Dutch and Huguenot settlers), uninvolved peoples, women and children in general, or German missionaries. That left only male colonists and the Schutzgruppe as targets. Leutwein then succeeded in convincing one of the rebel tribes to surrender their weapons. Apparently, that was a deceptive and treacherous tactic, because he then also requested military help from Berlin.

At that point, the kaiser was in control of the government and the Imperial German Army, and his reaction was predictable. Leutwein wanted a peace treaty, but the kaiser had no interest in such a weak response. He sent the experienced Army Lieutenant-General Lothar von Trotha and an expeditionary force of 1,400 troops on June 11, 1904. Trotha reported to the German General Staff, who reported directly to the kaiser. Leutwein wanted a political settlement, but Trotha had other ideas. In government communiqués, he said, "My intimate knowledge of many central African nations (Bantu and others) has everywhere convinced me of the necessity that the Negro does not respect treaties but only brute force. . . . I believe that the nation as such should be annihilated, or, if this was not possible by tactical measures, have to be expelled from the country. . . . This will be possible if the water-holes from Grootfontein to Gobabis are occupied. The constant movement of our troops will enable us to find the small groups of this nation who have moved backward and destroy them gradually."

THE BATTLE OF WATERBERG

Leutwein remained in command of the German forces until Trotha could get organized. Trotha took over on June 11, 1904, and Leutwein was then basically out of the picture. At the outset of the battle, the Germans fielded 1,500 troops, while the Hereros numbered almost 6,000 warriors with perhaps 50,000 additional supporting native families. But in terms of weaponry, the Hereros were drastically outclassed. The Germans were armed with 1,625 modern rifles, thirty pieces of artillery, and fourteen machine guns, while the Hereros depended mainly on mounted forces armed with close-combat weaponry, with scattered modern armaments. But the Hereros had no plan of attack and were awaiting a peace negotiation to be tendered by Leutwein. Whereas Trotha spent June, July, and early August supplying his forces at the expected site of battle with weaponry and munitions sent from the railhead to the battlefield by oxcart. By early August, the Herero's mounted infantry occupied the Waterberg Military Station but were mainly bunched together in a corner of the Waterberg plateau, while the German troops were organizing on the plateau. Trotha's plan was to force the Hereros off the plateau from the east and west and to squeeze them toward waiting German columns in the south and southeast, and thus surround and entrap them. The Germans would then attempt to annihilate the Hereros with attacks from all sides.

On August 11, the official date of the Battle of Waterberg, the Herero forces were quickly defeated by the German machine guns and artillery. However, the German commander of the southeastern column failed to maneuver into position in time and did not inform Trotha. This opened up a gap, which caused the western column to continue eastward past their line of demarcation and to push the Hereros off the plateau and out into the desert. This allowed the bulk of the Herero forces, along with their families and cattle, to escape the trap and move out into the Kalahari Desert. But instead of being a relief from the battle, this turned out to be a fate worse than a quick death by machine-gun fire.

THE MURDER OF SURVIVORS

Trotha's men quickly pursued the Hereros out into the desert to kill any survivors. According to Wikipedia, "The pursuing German forces prevented groups of Hereros from breaking from the main body of the fleeing force and pushed them further into the desert. As exhausted Hereros fell to the ground, unable to go on, German soldiers, acting on orders, killed men, women, and children." In his 1980 book *Let Us Die Fighting: The Struggle of the Herero and Nama against German Imperialism (1884–1915)*, Horst Dreschler quotes Jan Cloete, a German guide who witnessed the atrocities. Cloete said, "I was present when the Hereros were defeated in a battle in the vicinity of Waterberg. After the battle all men, women, and children who fell into German hands, wounded or otherwise, were mercilessly put to death. Then the Germans set off in pursuit of the rest, and all those found by the wayside and in the sandveld were shot down and bayoneted to death. The mass of the Herero men were unarmed and thus unable to offer resistance. They were just trying to get away with their cattle."

Fig. 5.1. German Namibia genocide

A small contingent of fewer than one thousand Hereros moved eastward out into the Omaheki Desert, eluding the pursuing Germans, and headed for Bechuanaland, which was a British territory. They succeeded in reaching the frontier and were granted asylum by the British. Trotha, perturbed that so many had avoided his massacre, ordered the desert sealed off. It should be realized that crossing the Kalahari was a major heroic accomplishment in itself. After that, there is evidence that Trotha ordered all the desert wells to be poisoned, in case any others tried to escape death by crossing the desert. German patrols later found skeletons around dry water holes, some as deep as forty-three feet, where the escaping Hereros had desperately sought to find water.

Trotha evidently was concerned about the effect on his military reputation in Berlin because of his failure to "annihilate" all the Hereros. Then, on October 2, he issued a stern proclamation to all the Hereros. He said:

> I, the great general of the German soldiers, send this letter to the Herero. The Herero are German subjects no longer. They have killed, stolen, cut off the ears and other parts of the body of wounded soldiers, and now are too cowardly to want to fight any longer. I announce to the people that whoever hands me one of the chiefs shall receive 1,000 marks, and 5,000 marks for Samuel Maharero. The Herero nation must now leave the country. If it refuses, I shall compel it to do so with the "long tube" (cannon). Any Herero found inside the German frontier, with or without a gun or cattle, will be executed. I shall spare neither women nor children. I shall give the order to drive them away and fire on them. Such are my words to the Herero people.

In a subsequent proclamation, Trotha elaborated on this announcement. He said that captured males were to be executed without exception, but women and children were to be driven into the desert, where they were to die more "humanely" by starvation or dehydration. This calculation about which type of death is more appropriate for women and children borders on the insane. It reveals the strange, self-deceptive thinking of the German men that resulted from the Archon/Reptilian programming. Already pridefully full of themselves because they had bought into the German racist and patriarchal propaganda, they had to find an explanation that allowed them to give some sort of strange priority to a courtly drawn-out death for women by starvation instead of by bullets to the head. But then, realizing how silly that argument was, Trotha went on to rationalize his decision by explaining that it really was a racial struggle after all and that women and children might "infect German troops with their diseases." He must have then realized how stupid *that* was because he did not condemn allowing his men to rape the women before they died, which was a rampant practice. So *still* unsatisfied with his rationalizations, he finally wrote in 1909, "If I had made the small water holes accessible to the womenfolk, I would run the risk of an African catastrophe comparable to the Battle of Beresonia." That was a strange and inappropriate comparison! During the Russian Campaign of 1812, the Russians actually helped the retreating French

*Fig. 5.2. General
Lothar von Trotha*

army by leaving one of the bridges over the Beresonia River to remain intact, by mistake, thus allowing the French Grand Army to escape a massacre by crossing the river. It could have been something that Hitler might have said about Dunkirk. For a German general to say that leaving some unarmed women and children alive would have been a catastrophe boggles the mind to the limit. It meant that they viewed the "failure to annihilate" as a disgrace! Those German men had been turned into inhuman zombies!

So the plan now was to deprive the fleeing natives of relief at the watering holes for themselves and their cattle. Most of the subsequent Herero deaths were caused by starvation and dehydration in the unforgiving desert.

AGREEMENT FROM BERLIN

Alfred von Schleiffen, the chief of the Imperial German General Staff, approved of Trotha's intentions, but wasn't sure about his methods. He agreed that it was a "racial struggle" and that it was necessary to "wipe out the entire nation, or to drive them out of the country." So much for the visionary German promises made in Brussels in 1890! This conclusion is another supreme example of the self-deluded thinking of the German military men. They had convinced themselves that it was perfectly all right to kick an entire population out of their own native land, going back many generations, because they believed that the white man deserved the land more than the black. The illogical arrogance of this position didn't even occur to them, testifying to the fact that they had been programmed by the Archons at a deep subconscious level without realizing it. But what is astounding is that they were prepared to adopt cruel and merciless measures to achieve their goal when they had more civilized options at their disposal. Again, this testifies to the Archontic influence, which seeks to breed fear and terror in the human race. They decided to put the Herero and Nama natives in concentration camps and work them to death! This amounted to creating a hell on Earth for these innocent souls. Even Leutwein, seemingly the most compassion-ate and "humane" of all of them, harbored more pragmatic motives. He wrote, "I do not concur with those fanatics who want to see the Herero destroyed altogether. . . . I would consider such a move a grave mistake from an economic point of view. We need the Herero as cattle breeders . . . and especially as laborers." So it seems that they were all cut from the same cloth.

6

The Herero Genocide

CONCENTRATION CAMPS

The Germans started sending Herero prisoners to their first concentration camp as early as March 1905. It was on an island in Lüderitz Bay on the Atlantic coast, connected to Lüderitz only by a single causeway. The camp was placed on a rocky peninsula at the far end of the small island, where the prisoners would have suffered complete exposure to the strong, cold winds that sweep Lüderitz for most of the year. This was Shark Island, the worst of the five concentration camps set up by the Germans. Right from the beginning, its staff became notorious for their brutal treatment of prisoners and it became known as "the Death Camp." By as early as May 1905, fifty-nine men, fifty-nine women, and seventy-three children had died at Shark Island. As its reputation spread among the Hereros, many potential prisoners killed themselves before they could be sent there.

As prisoners arrived at the camp, they were categorized as "fit" or "unfit" for work, but both groups were forced into some degree of slave labor for the German military or for settlers, and death certificates were issued upon arrival, meaning none were expected to leave alive. The certificates were preprinted, showing "death by exhaustion following privation." One can easily discern from this the seeds of the modus operandi of the Nazi concentration camps forty years later. They were the result of the same inhuman Archontic mentality.

Food in the camps was extremely scarce, mostly just rice with no added ingredients. Since the prisoners had no pots and pans, the rice remained uncooked, and consequently, it was indigestible. Horses and oxen that died in the camp were given to the inmates as food. Diseases were rampant. Dysentery and lung diseases were common. Despite their weakened condition, the Hereros were taken outside the camp every day for labor, under harsh treatment by the German guards, while the sick were left without any medical assistance or nursing care.

Food for the Sharks

According to Wikipedia, Shark Island was aptly named. Frederick Carruthers Cornell was an English soldier, geologist, prospector, and author born in Devon, England, and educated at the Bedford School. Cornell is best known for his wartime activities during the Boer War, the Maritz Rebellion, and the First World War, as well as for his publications. In 1902, he came to South Africa and displayed great interest in Namaqua land. He was an editor of the *Cape Register*. His publications include a 1920 volume of reminiscences, *The Glamour of Prospecting*, which has become an important eyewitness account of the Herero and Namaqua Genocide by the Germans between 1904 and 1908. Cornell wrote about the Shark Island camp: "Cold—for the nights are often bitterly cold there—hunger, thirst, exposure, disease and madness claimed scores of victims every day, and cartloads of their bodies were every day carted over to the back beach, buried in a few inches of sand at low tide, and as the tide came in, the bodies went out, food for the sharks." Cornell was ultimately awarded the Order of the British Empire for his military service.

In September 1905, the *Cape Argus*, a South African newspaper, reported a story by an employee of the camp. In his report he said, "The women who are captured and not executed are set to work for the military as prisoners. . . . [I] saw numbers of them at Angra Pequena [i.e., Lüderitz] put to the hardest work, and so starved that they were nothing but skin and bones. They are given hardly anything to eat, and I have very often seen them pick up bits of refuse food thrown away by the transport riders. If they are caught doing so, they are *sjamboked* [beaten with a rhinoceros-hide whip]." August Kuhlmann, one of the first civilians to visit the camp, wrote in September 1905 about what he observed there. "A woman, who was so weak from illness that she could not stand, crawled to some of the other prisoners to beg for water. The overseer fired five shots at her. Two shots hit her: one in the thigh, the other smashing her forearm . . . in the night she died."

Shootings, hangings, beatings with the sjambok, and other harsh treatment of the forced laborers were common. In another article in the *Cape Argus,* dated September 28, 1905, with the heading "In German S. W. Africa: Further Startling Allegations: Horrible Cruelty," some of the abuses were described. Percival Griffith, an accountant and transport worker at Angra Pequena, related what he observed:

> There are hundreds of them, mostly women and children and a few old men . . . when they fall they are sjamboked by the soldiers in charge of the gang, with full force, until they get up. . . . On one occasion I saw a woman carrying a child of under a year old slung on her back, and with a heavy sack of grain on her head . . . she fell. The corporal sjamboked her for certainly more than four minutes and sjamboked the baby as well . . . the woman struggled slowly to her feet, and went on with her load. She did not utter a sound the whole time, but the baby cried very hard.

The pitiful, starved, gaunt condition of the Herero women didn't stop the prison guards from using them for prostitution. It was the only way the poor creatures could eat real food. The utter depths of the remorseless German cruelty shown there is, even now, after the horrors of Nazi Germany, still incredible.

Medical Experiments

As if the brutal treatment of the prisoners was not enough, the German doctors also used them for medical research. Prisoners who were suffering with scurvy were injected with experimental toxic substances, including arsenic and opium, to study the postmortem effects by autopsy if they died or to study their recoveries if they survived. Also, German zoologists were interested in analysis of body parts of the recently deceased. Three hundred skulls were sent to Germany for studies of racial characteristics. It seems they weren't yet through with this strange obsession during World War II, when more skulls from concentration camp victims were studied. After years of talks, twenty skulls were returned to Namibia for burial, and an additional fourteen were repatriated from the University of Freiburg where, presumably, they had been on display.

Slavery

With the closure of the concentration camps, all surviving Hereros were distributed as laborers for settlers in the German colony. From that time on, all Hereros over the age of seven were forced to wear a metal disc with their labor registration number and were banned from owning land or cattle, a necessity for a free pastoral society. So this once proud people, now decimated, were reduced to becoming slaves in their own land.

The Deaths

There are various estimates of the number of Hereros who died in the first decade of the twentieth century. According to the Whitaker Report, produced by the Human Rights Council of the United Nations in 1985 the original population of eighty thousand Hereros alive in 1903 was reduced to fifteen thousand "starving refugees" by 1907. So sixty-five thousand were killed over a three-year period. This tallies with various newspaper reports from 2004, when Germany finally acknowledged that the Herero decimation during that period was actually the first genocide of the twentieth century. The council reported on several other genocides that followed in the twentieth century, of which, of course, the Nazi slaughter of six million Jews in the concentration camps in the 1940s was by far the worst.

German Casualties and Cost

About nineteen thousand German troops were engaged in the conflict, of which three thousand saw combat. The rest were used for upkeep and administration. The German losses were 676 soldiers killed in combat, 76 missing, and 689 dead from disease. The Equestrian Monument at Windhoek in Namibia was erected in 1912 to celebrate the "victory" and to remember the fallen Germans, with no mention of the slaughtered indigenous population. It remains a bone of contention in independent Namibia. After much controversy over the years in independent Namibia, the statue was taken down permanently in 2013, and put in storage in the Alte Feste, a former fortress that is now a museum, at the same site.

The campaign had cost Germany 600 million marks. The normal annual subsidy to the colony was 14.5 million marks. In 1908, diamonds were discovered in the territory, and this did much to boost its prosperity, though it was short-lived.

In 1915, at the start of World War I, the German colony was taken over and occupied in the Southwest Africa Campaign by the Union of South Africa, acting on behalf of the British Imperial Government. South Africa received a League of Nations mandate over Southwest Africa in 1919 under the Treaty of Versailles.

7
A Century of War

The advent of the kaiser to power in 1888 began a new era for Germany. Despite the fact that the kaiser claimed to be indebted to Bismarck for how he had transformed the Prussian states into a strong, unified Germany and increased Germany's wealth and global influence, he nevertheless harbored the belief that Bismarck was not strong enough and did not go far enough in showing the world how great and mighty Germany could be. This was the kaiser's obsession. Now that he was on the world's stage, the kaiser's malnourished ego demanded that he become front and center and be appreciated by the rest of the world, and he was prepared to go to great lengths to make that impression. On the surface, he appeared to be modest, civilized, and tolerant, but he was really anything but, and his "inner tiger" frequently emerged, but in a very controlled manner. And when it did emerge, many people died. So it didn't take long after the kaiser's coronation for the two men to clash. By 1890, Bismarck, although still vital and strong at age seventy-five, could not deal with the stealthy ambition of the kaiser for a new path of world worship of Germany, and thereby of himself. So, as previously noted, Bismarck stepped aside, reluctantly resigned the chancellorship, clearly pushed out by the kaiser. Kaiser Wilhelm's father, King Frederick III, had not interfered with Bismarck's rule and had been more of a figurehead.

It was an Englishman who first recognized the inner kaiser. Sir Edward Grey, British foreign secretary from 1905 to 1916, understood well his ambitions. Grey wrote in November 1908, "He is like a battle-ship with steam up and screws going, but with no rudder, and he will run into something someday and cause a catastrophe. He has the strongest army in the world and the Germans don't like being laughed at, and are looking for somebody on whom to vent their temper and use their strength." Wilhelm's ascendancy to becoming emperor "just happened" to coincide with the maturing of the new generation of young men who had been programmed by the Archons and were now veterans of the Herero conflict and ready and able to participate in any "inner tiger" requirement for a fighting force. So the kaiser had a clear path ahead to realize his military plans, no matter how bold, and he knew it because he had prepared for this convergence.

THE OFFICER CORPS

In his memoirs, Kaiser Wilhelm says:

My close relations with the army are a matter of common knowledge. In this direction I conformed to the tradition of my family. Prussia's kings did not chase cosmopolitan mirages, but realized that the welfare of their land could only be assured by means of a real power protecting industry and commerce. If, in a number of utterances, I admonished my people to "keep their powder dry and their swords sharp," the warning was addressed alike to foe and friend. I wished our foes to pause and think a long time before they dared to engage with us. I wished to cultivate a manly spirit in the German people; I wished to make sure that, when the enemy hour struck for us to defend the fruits of our industry against an enemy's lust of conquest, it should find a strong race.

This is not the comment of a peace-loving leader. It is a jingoistic throwing down of the gauntlet of military challenge to anyone who dares to think of challenging the kaiser.

In support of my thesis that the kaiser relied on the men of the generation that we have identified, he confirmed this when he said:

> In view of its proud duty as an educator and leader of the nation in arms, the officer corps occupied a particularly important position in the German Empire. . . . I entered much and willingly in relations with the officer corps and felt like a comrade among them . . . it must be admitted that nowhere else were self-discipline, fidelity to duty, and simplicity cultivated to such an extent as among the officers. A process of weeding out such as existed in no other profession allowed only the ablest and best to reach positions of influence. The commanding generals were men of a high degree of attainment and ability and—what is even more important—men of character. It is a difficult matter to single out individuals from among them.

It may be recalled that we previously noted that men of this age group, those murderers of defenseless Herero natives, would be of officer age in time for World War I. And it was Wilhelm who had sent the racist Lieutenant-General von Trotha to do the killing of the Hereros.

THE BRYCE REPORT

I made the case in my last book, *Alien World Order,* that it was the kaiser who had started World War I and had approved the slaughter and the brutalities by his vaunted officer corps as they marched, virtually unopposed, through Belgium and killed and enslaved hundreds of thousands of innocent Belgian civilians. These atrocities were revealed and cataloged in the *Report of the Committee on Alleged German Outrages,* or *The Bryce Report,* produced by the British in May 1915. The German Army used Belgium as a corridor to attack France. Allegedly, they first demanded unopposed passage through Belgium on August 2, 1914, but Belgium refused the request. Germany then invaded Belgium on the very next day, on August 3, thereby violating the Treaty of London of

1839, in which Belgium was guaranteed neutrality by all the European powers. Germany then declared war on France the very same day. Clearly, the Germans were poised for the invasion regardless of the Belgian reply.

THE SINKING OF THE *LUSITANIA*

The German atrocities in Belgium in August 1914 were discussed at length in *Alien World Order* in the chapter titled "The Rape of Belgium." *The Bryce Report* was instrumental in motivating the United States to enter into the war, but not until two years after its publication. Whereas the British declared war on Germany the day after Germany invaded Belgium, on August 4, based on German violation of the Treaty of London. But the United States' determination to declare war on Germany was further encouraged by the sinking of the British luxury passenger liner *Lusitania* in British waters (see plate 4) off the southern coast of Ireland, five days after *The Bryce Report* was published in May 1915. There were 1,192 deaths, of which 125 were of United States citizens. Under the existing Cruiser Rules of naval warfare, commercial and passenger ships were to be warned of imminent sinking, permitting the passengers to first escape in lifeboats. But the kaiser allowed his naval commander Admiral Alfred von Tirpitz to adopt a policy of unrestricted submarine warfare against enemy vessels of all types in the British war zone in February 1915. So that meant that all ships flying the British flag in that zone could be sunk without warning. However, a warning had been posted by the German embassy at the Cunard Line's passenger terminal in New York before the *Lusitania* sailed. But the British admiralty believed that the *Lusitania* was too fast to be caught, especially if warned by radio. So the *Lusitania's* captain understood the dangers. It was definitely a risky proposition. Apparently, the captain of the U-boat U-20, which sank the ship with a single torpedo, understood what he was doing because he had identified the ship. He clearly had seen the four smokestacks of the ship, which was comparable in size to the *Titanic,* from only seven hundred meters on a clear, sunny day. So he knew he was killing more than a thousand civilians.

However, he was following the orders of von Tirpitz. But von Tirpitz did nothing without the approval of the kaiser, especially since the kaiser was known to be heavily invested in naval warfare. He had admired and envied the British fleet ever since he was a boy. It was at his insistence that the German Naval Law of 1908 had been passed to give Germany a real navy. And it was followed by four additional naval laws up to the outbreak of the war, culminating in an awesome German fleet of warships that could almost challenge the British fleet. So the blame for the deaths of the *Lusitania* passengers must rest squarely on the kaiser, who had permitted the adoption of the policy of unrestricted submarine warfare that previous February. That policy was rescinded shortly after the *Lusitania* debacle because of world outrage.

Still, U.S. President Woodrow Wilson resisted joining the European war, despite American ties to both England and France. It wasn't until two years later, when in February 1917 the Germans again instituted unrestricted U-boat warfare in the Atlantic, thus endangering U.S. commercial and passenger vessels, that Wilson had enough and declared war on Germany.

A GERMAN SUBCONTINENT

One has to marvel at the colossal ego of the kaiser to try to defeat France and Russia so that he would then rule the entire western Eurasian subcontinent. That had to be his goal. Evidently, he believed it was possible because of his arrangement with the Krupp family (see pages 72–78) and therefore his inexhaustible supply of superweaponry. And, of course, he now had a formidable navy and even a decent air force that included such air aces as Manfred von Richthofen, known as the Red Baron, as well as twenty-nine blimp airships for reconnaissance and bombing. In view of his experience with concentration camps in Namibia, he would, no doubt, place these camps all over Europe and

Russia to dispose of his political enemies in the same horrible, sadistic manner that he had employed with the Hereros. The kaiser was basically an early version of Adolf Hitler!

And to complete this comparison, the kaiser's anti-Semitism should be addressed. While Wilhelm did have some Jewish friends who moved in his social circles, they were mainly men who had influence and whom he could use. But his anti-Semitism was fervent and well known. He was a great admirer of Houston Stewart Chamberlain, who was notoriously anti-Semitic. Chamberlain's 1899 book, *The Foundations of the Nineteenth Century,* was an anti-Semitic diatribe. The kaiser's admiration of Chamberlain was so great that it moved him to extend an invitation for him to come to Potsdam to meet the empress, and he corresponded with Chamberlain for over a decade. According to Lamar Cecil in his biography of Wilhelm, *Wilhelm II: Emperor and Exile, 1900–1941,* "For individual Jews, ranging from rich businessmen and major art collectors to purveyors of elegant goods in Berlin stores, he had considerable esteem, but he prevented Jewish citizens from having careers in the army and the diplomatic corps and frequently used abusive language against them."

KRUPP

The industries of most concern to the Reptilian overlords in the early twentieth century were weaponry, pharmaceuticals, and the media. Consequently, they convinced the Bavarian Illuminati to focus on those areas at that time and had them divert huge sums of money to the right groups. They then contacted key individuals in those groups and helped them along by influence from their home in the Fourth Dimension, better known as the lower astral realm. Of these three critical industries, weaponry took first place because a world war was tops on their agenda. Consequently, early in the twentieth century, Germany became the largest worldwide manufacturer of weaponry of all types. This was accomplished almost exclusively through a single corporate entity owned outright by the Krupp family. Wikipedia offers the most succinct summation of this phenomenon.

> The Krupp family, a prominent 400-year-old German dynasty from Essen, has become famous for their production of steel, artillery, ammunition, and other armaments. The family business, known as Friedrich Krupp AG, was the largest company in Europe at the beginning of the 20th century. It was important to weapons development and production in both world wars. One of the most powerful dynasties in European history, for 400 years, Krupp flourished as the premier weapons manufacturer for Germany. From the Thirty Years' War until the end of the Second World War, they produced everything from battleships, U-boats, tanks, howitzers, guns, utilities, and hundreds of other commodities.

So a single German corporation had the unique power to carry out the Reptilian war agenda by creating products for the slaughter of millions of the human population. Needless to say, this sudden and extensive rearmament of Germany alarmed the other nations in Europe, who were already very concerned about German militancy, and so they felt it necessary to rearm also. So, naturally, they turned to Krupp, the preeminent arms manufacturer in Europe, further enriching the coffers of the Krupp family.

A STRATEGIC MARRIAGE

The Krupp company remained under autocratic male family rule until 1903, when only a teenaged girl remained to lead the family and the massive corporation. Bertha, the oldest daughter of Friedrich Alfred Krupp, inherited all but four shares of the now joint-stock corporation. Because weaponry was so vital to the burgeoning war plans of Kaiser Wilhelm II, he arranged for Bertha to marry a man of his choice to run the company. The man he chose, Gustav von Bohlen und Halbach, a Prussian diplomat employed at the Vatican, was obviously someone the kaiser knew he could manipulate. So thereby, the kaiser became the sole master of the German armaments industry as he prepared to attack Russia and France. That meant that the kaiser could now select the recipients of Krupp's best armaments, including the enemies of Germany who relied heavily on Krupp products. That ability played out precisely as planned, so that by 1911, 50 percent of all Krupp armaments were sold to Germany, and fifty-two other nations had to divide up what was left. And that remainder could easily be strategically sliced up further to deny weaponry based on battlefield conditions.

This marriage of Bertha Krupp to Gustav von Bohlen und Halbach sealed the horrible, blood-soaked fate of Europe, and ultimately the entire world, for the twentieth century. At the wedding, the kaiser announced that he was awarding the additional name Krupp to von Bohlen und Halbach by imperial decree and that name would now be passed on to all the descendants of the couple. So, by this matrimonial sleight of hand, the kaiser ensured that the historic Krupp legacy would live on and that he would continue to be in control of armaments in his role as the self-styled "godfather" of the chief executive of the company.

Fig. 7.1. Gustav von Bohlen und Halbach, circa 1931

Fig. 7.2. Bertha Krupp

BIG BERTHA AND BIGGER KRUPP

Von Bohlen und Halbach (now Gustav Krupp von Bohlen und Halbach) has been described as "an avowed monarchist." This explains his close friendship with the kaiser. He was thirty-six when he was persuaded by the kaiser to marry the twenty-year-old Bertha Krupp, which probably wasn't very difficult since she was much younger, very attractive, and popular in Berlin haute society. At that stage of his life, Krupp von Bohlen und Halbach's political leanings had probably become hardened. However, no one could have predicted just how "avowed" he would become in later life. Monarchism, especially the absolute version, is a belief that an absolute ruler should have unrestricted power to govern a nation. Based on that philosophy, Krupp von Bohlen und Halbach was more than pleased to help the monarch, in the person of the kaiser, build Germany into a fearsome superpower, armed to the teeth, that could take over Europe. The weaponry produced by Krupp under Krupp von Bohlen und Halbach's leadership was astounding, and since he had the power to deprive Germany's adversaries of equal capability, it seemed to the kaiser that the path to Germany's hegemony over the European continent was assured. This belief emboldened him to be willing to fight a two-front war, despite Napoleon's failure to succeed at that strategy.

It was especially in artillery that Germany excelled. Krupp designed a battlefield megaweapon called the Gamma-Gerät howitzer, which weighed 150 tons and fired shells weighing up to 1,160 kilograms (2,557 pounds). But it had to be fired while embedded in concrete from a stationary fortification. Wikipedia says, "It had to be transported in sections on ten railway cars—six for the gun and another four for the bedding." However, the kaiser wanted something more mobile to meet true battlefield conditions, so the Krupp engineers designed a new model. Again, we learn from Wikipedia:

> The new howitzer was a road-mobile weapon mounted on a two-wheeled, field-type carriage of conventional construction. It was a completely different weapon from the Gamma-Gerät. The barrel was shorter than Gamma's by four calibers length, and reverted to the conventional Krupp sliding-wedge breech. With thinner walls, the barrel was of generally lighter construction than Gamma's and fired lighter shells of around 830 kg. Fully assembled it weighed 43 tons, much less than Gamma, and did not have to be emplaced in concrete. Special steel "mats" were developed, onto which the wheels were driven, with a steel aiming arc at the rear of the carriage that allowed limited traverse. This aiming arc was fitted with a massive "spade" that was buried in the ground and which helped anchor the weapon. To prevent the weapon bogging down in muddy roads the guns were equipped with Radgürteln, feet attached to the rim of the wheels to reduce ground pressure. Krupp and Daimler developed a tractor for [the Bertha] this model, though Podeus motorploughs were also used to tow the guns, which were broken down into five loads when on the road.

It was this model that became known as the legendary "Big Bertha," and it wreaked incredible damage on the Allied fortifications and

Fig. 7.3. "Big Bertha"

armies, especially in Belgium, where the fortress wall constructions had used older non-steel-backed concrete materials.

Just as World War II was largely a war of aerial bombardments, World War I was largely a battle of field artillery, and so the role of Krupp weaponry was of prime importance, although the French artillery was not far behind. In the massive and famous Battle of Verdun, the ten-month stalemate in 1916, there were over seven hundred thousand casualties in total, of which about 70 percent were the result of artillery fire, almost equally divided between the French and German forces.

Fig. 7.4. Gustav Krupp von Bohlen und Halbach shaking the hand of Adolf Hitler

Even though he lost the war, the kaiser had completed his Reptilian mission by laying the groundwork for the advent of Hitler. He had organized and improved the military, created the navy, of which the submarine fleet was paramount in World War II, prepared the German people for a continuation of a monarchical form of government for the twentieth century, which Hitler then could take advantage of, created the false mythos of the "Versailles stab in the back" concept, which Hitler used very effectively to sell the German populace on the need for war, caused the slaughter of a generation of young men in the militaries of the Allied nations, which would take time to replace, and most importantly, created the Krupp weapons dynasty, which would prove to be critical to Hitler's blitzkrieg war strategy.

8

A New Rome

After the war, it was primarily the right-wing parties in Germany that were the most vocal about the so-called betrayal of the Treaty of Versailles in 1919, which was a fiction. These complaints were voiced mainly by the Prussian monarchist elements in Germany, of which Krupp von Bohlen und Halbach was a leading figure. Consequently, he was most anxious for a rematch, especially since his company had the most to gain in such a renewal of hostilities. Anticipating a resurgence of German militarism, he was driven by this conviction to commence a sub-rosa rearmament after 1919, in violation of the Treaty of Versailles, while he and others sought the right candidate for restoration of the monarchy. However, in 1933, he became convinced that Adolf Hitler should be the leader of the new Germany. Once committed to Hitler, Krupp von Bohlen und Halbach was motivated to drive the Krupp organization at a furious pace to produce weaponry, and thus, after six years of an all-out manufacturing effort as well as energetic general industrial leadership, he was ready to present to Hitler the most advanced slate of armaments in the world for land, sea, and air, when Hitler began hostilities in 1939. It was this incredible effort that made the famous Nazi blitzkrieg and the early victories in Western Europe possible.

Without Krupp's enthusiastic support, it is unlikely that Hitler could ever have achieved his rulership of the German people. Krupp also recruited other top industrialists to this cause so that the financial needs of the Nazi Party were never a problem. In a letter written to Hjalmar Schacht, the president of the Reichsbank, dated May 3, 1933, he said:

> As Dr. Hoettgen and I had the opportunity of mentioning to you yesterday, it is proposed to initiate a collection in the most far-reaching circles of German industry, including agriculture and the banking world, which is to be put at the disposal of the Füehrer of the NSDAP in the name of "The Hitler Fund," which would replace collections in many cases separately organized of the various NSDAP organizations and the Stahlhelm. It has been decided to appoint a management council for this central collection; I have accepted the chairmanship of the management council at the unanimous request of the principal federations, inspired by the wish to collaborate with my full strength in this task, which is to be a symbol of gratitude to the Füehrer of the nation.

Ultimately, the Hitler Fund made Hitler very rich, and he was able to use the money to live comfortably in Argentina after the war.

Such devotion was especially strange since Hitler had absolutely no credentials to have merited such praise. But even though he was not of royal blood, Hitler did indeed personify the Prussian ideal, and that was enough for Krupp. In order for Hitler to become the national leader, the German political system had to adopt the concept of *Führerprinzip* and to abandon democracy. According to Wikipedia:

> The Führerprinzip (German for "leader principle") prescribed the fundamental basis of political authority in the governmental structures of the Third Reich. This principle can be most succinctly understood to mean that "the Führer's word is above all written law" and that governmental policies, decisions, and offices ought to work toward the realization of this end. In actual political usage, it refers mainly to the practice of dictatorship within the ranks of a politi-

cal party itself, and as such, it has become an earmark of political fascism.

Hitler had achieved that position within the Nazi Party by resigning from the party until they had granted him that status. According to the principle of Führerprinzip, every leader demands absolute obedience from those below him in the chain of authority and answers only to those above him. This required obedience even over concerns of right and wrong. Hitler himself, as the supreme leader, answered only to God and the German people. But after achieving this party leadership, Hitler declared, "In this hour, I was responsible for the fate of the German nation and was therefore the supreme judge of the German people!"

The achievement of such a position in modern society is basically a throwback to Roman political organization, wherein only the emperor had such absolute power. But even in Rome, which was really a republic, only Julius Caesar had himself proclaimed a "dictator in perpetuity." So essentially, Hitler achieved Caesarian stature, and that is why he demanded a *sieg heil* from the entire populace (see plate 5). No national leader in modern times, even the kaiser, had ever reached such Olympian heights.

The infusion of Führerprinzip into the Nazi Party in 1919 was largely due to the fact that the party, at that time, attracted unemployed veterans of World War I who had followed the kaiser. These were all fighting men who had been born in the generation we have identified as having been programmed by the Archons and Reptilians. So strict hierarchical training had been easily bred into them in the kaiser's military ranks. These men constituted the Freikorps in postwar Germany, which became the backbone of the Nazi Party.

KRUPP VON BOHLEN UND HALBACH'S COMMITMENT TO HITLER

Krupp von Bohlen und Halbach's commitment to Hitler was total. Like so many others, he was mesmerized by Hitler's oratory, so carefully calculated to attract businessmen and even the intellectuals. In a speech dated October 27, 1935, Krupp von Bohlen und Halbach said, "Our thoughts fly therefore by themselves in this festive hour of our plant community, to the man whom we thank for the resurrection of our Nation: Adolf Hitler, the patron of German labor and German art. Unanimously we will confess and pledge ourselves to stand behind the Füehrer and his movement today and forever and thereby to be of service to the idea of eternal Germany." Such excesses of devotion to Hitler were not uncommon in those balmy early days of Germany's revival. Hitler had practiced his ability to hypnotize the populace, and he had honed it to perfection. In another speech, on May 1, 1936, after the German occupation of the Rhineland, Krupp stated:

> Never has a statesman fought for the soul of his people and for its well-being with such faith, such ardor, such endurance. We shall never forget how deeply we are indebted to him. I only mention here the abolition of the parties and the unification of the people, the regaining of the sovereignty in the Rhineland, the extensive abolition of unemployment, the accomplishments of the labor service, the magnificent public buildings, the roads, bridges, and canals [which were soon to be reduced to ashes during the war]. The world will have to get used to the fact that the voice of the Füehrer is the voice of the whole German people.

But Krupp von Bohlen und Halbach didn't stop there in his effusive devotion to the führer. He went on, "Jubileers and co-workers! We shall be thankful to fate that we were and are permitted to be eye and action witnesses of the great turning point in our German history, and we shall thank especially the divine destiny that it has presented us with a man like Adolf Hitler. Let us then combine all that which moves our hearts upon mention of this name into the cry: Our people and fatherland and its great Füehrer Adolf Hitler. Sieg Heil!"

Fig. 8.1. The Nazi regime was, in many ways, a reincarnation of Imperial Rome in Nazi Germany.

ALFRIED KRUPP TAKES OVER

As World War II advanced, Krupp von Bohlen und Halbach developed health problems, and Alfried, the eldest of the eight children of Gustav and Bertha, took over control of the firm in 1943. Alfried Krupp's production goals became huge as Hitler's tanks and artillery were chewed up at Stalingrad and on the western front and as the Krupp factories were decimated from the air. So he turned to the option that the Illuminati always keep in reserve and that was infused into the Nazi Party, outright slavery.

An internet source titled "Fritz Springmeier and His Work," says "Fritz Springmeier is probably the world's foremost authority on the bloodlines of the Illuminati and the techniques they employ to create a mind controlled slave." His seminal book on this subject is a three-volume work that is widely quoted, and has been available on Amazon for almost twenty years. In his internet essay "The Krupps and the Illuminati," taken from the article "13 Bloodlines of the Illuminati," he says:

> During W.W. II, the Krupps took tens of thousands of Jews and other people and used them as slave labor. A concentration camp at Buschmannshof, Germany, was created for the babies of Krupp's slave labor. The babies who were sent to this concentration camp would then die of starvation and disease. The slaves of the Krupps during W.W. II were tortured in small boxes, whipped etc., etc. However, the politically correct line today in Germany is that the Krupps were made to do this by the Nazis. And that politically correct line is a fabricated lie, because numerous documents show that the Krupps went to the Nazi government and begged for slaves to work in their factories, and that the Krupps intentionally set up extremely harsh working conditions for their slaves. In fact, letters exist that show the Krupps couldn't get enough supply of torture weapons to use on their slaves.

But then the workers for Krupp have always worked under serf conditions. A visitor to a Krupp factory said, "For all practical purposes the people of Essen are body and soul the property of the Krupps." At times the Krupps have been viewed as god figures by some of their workers. The foreign slaves in Germany were often looked on as less than human by many of the German people. That is the power of control and propaganda. The Krupps tried to burn mountains of records before the Allies captured their factories.

LESS THAN SLAVES

Alfried Krupp's conscienceless Illuminati bloodline became obvious in his World War II governance of the Krupp factories. That same internet article says further:

The massive trial documents of the Nuremberg trial of Alfried Krupp were never printed in Germany, and even today the truth about Krupp is unknown. History was rewritten by the controlled presses to make Alfried Krupp out to be the victim of Nazism, rather than to tell the truth about how he ran the Krupp empire beginning in 1943, and was actively involved in the rape & pillage of many nations, and actively involved in the torture of countless slave laborers who came from nations all over the world (anybody the Nazis found to arrest). The slaves who worked for Krupp were not even slaves. Hitler had made a law that slaves were to be fed so much per day according to how hard the work was that they had to do. Krupp's slaves were starved to death while being forced to do hard labor. There was an acute shortage of slaves to work and drastic needs for tanks, ships, artillery, subs, and other Krupp-produced weapons, so there was no logical reason for Krupp's personal factory guards to starve and beat slaves to death on a regular manner. The horrendous abuse that the slaves received actually often prevented the Krupp factories from being successful in their production goals. Slaves are generally fed and taken care of so they can work, but Krupp's slaves were not even given the basics that a slave gets—they were less than slaves, or as one slave who worked for Krupp said that as Krupp's slaves they didn't even have the status of "slave" but were like pieces of sandpaper to be used and discarded.

Krupp's slaves were the worst treated in Germany and frequently failed to achieve the production that was wanted due to the total dehumanization and horrible abuse systematically heaped on them. Slaves were tortured in the basement of Krupp's Hauptverwaltungsgebäude (the executive corporation office building in Essen). Unimpeachable witnesses declared that some of the most revolting torture of slaves occurred within earshot of Krupp's office. The secretaries who worked with Krupp could hear the screams of people being tortured, and there is no doubt that if they could hear them, Krupp could too, but he always ignored the screams with a stonelike face, as he did later during satanic rituals. One Illuminati survivor of those horrors remembers Krupp's distinctive face. Later, John J. McCloy, head of the Council on Foreign Relations and a member of the Illuminati, was given the job of high commissioner over occupied Germany. He overturned the Nuremberg trial decisions, stepped out of line with legalities, and freed Krupp from prison and exonerated him of "war guilt." The trial of Krupp's World War II war crimes had taken five years and produced 330,000 pages of court transcripts. All that work was swept aside by McCloy—a generational satanist himself, like Krupp. Krupp had thirty-seven of the best lawyers, who had given more than a good fight. They pulled every trick in the book for their client—including murdering witnesses, suppressing evidence, and so forth. The establishment newspapers in Europe and the United States portrayed Krupp as having not been allowed adequate legal help! (Nothing could be further from the truth; he was the "best-defended" Nuremberg criminal.)

Yet the evidence against Krupp was overwhelming, and the five Nuremberg judges had sentenced him to prison. The judges also had sentenced that all his possessions be taken from him. This was more than fair considering all the pillage and looting Krupp had personally directed throughout Europe. The British and American governments never carried out the judges' orders to take Krupp's property away, and after serving awhile in prison (having a vacation from his company workload), the Illuminati set him free. Krupp was made out to be a martyr in the press, which claimed he was the only Nazi who had property confiscated (which was a lie by the press) so that it looked like he'd been singled out for special victimization by the Nuremberg court. While he looked to the public like a victim for losing his property, none of it was ever taken away! This is a glaring example of how the Illuminati look after each other because they are all under the command of the Reptilians.

GALACTIC SLAVERY

This widespread adoption of slavery in German industrial organizations, which was notorious in the case of Krupp, is further evidence, in addition to Führerprinzip, that Nazi Germany itself was a throwback to imperial Rome, where slavery was institutionalized. It was all part of a national reincarnation of pagan society, led by the Nazi Party, which the German people easily fell into. They even had pagan rituals and parades in which the marchers were all dressed in authentic Roman garb. Even the "Hail Caesar" salute became normalized across all classes. It was truly a strange spectacle in the twentieth century and was ridiculed by the American press and moviemakers like Walt Disney. In any case, as we will see, the adoption of slavery in all German organizations was carried over to Base 211 in Antarctica, to which they brought thirty-six thousand slaves from occupied Europe, and then to their extraterrestrial colonies on the moon, Mars, Titan (a moon of Saturn), the asteroid Ceres, asteroids in the Kuiper Belt, and elsewhere in the galaxy.

BIG PHARMA

Perhaps even more significant were the German scientific advances in the pharmaceutical industry. This was of major importance since the Reptilians are known to be master bioengineers and biogeneticists. They use these skills to develop advanced programs in hybridization with targeted populations, and consequently, they require the same scientific expertise in the Illuminati industries that they work through. This was a perfect match with the German scientists, who were also known to have focused on development of advanced bioengineering. There are currently over 270 biotech companies in Germany, some of which are the largest and most advanced in the world, with branches and outlets all over the globe. IG Farben, the German chemical company that produced the poison gas Zyklon B, which was used to kill prisoners at Auschwitz and other concentration camps during

World War II, was, at one time, the largest company in Europe and the largest chemical and pharmaceutical company in the world. After World War II, when forced by the Allies to break up and to divest some of their companies, Farben spun off Bayer AG but retained several former Farben executives on the board of directors. Bayer has since become the sixteenth largest pharmaceutical company in the world as of 2015. Bayer is now also into crop science and has recently acquired the massive Monsanto Company, which is currently under fire for creating such soil-poisoning agricultural chemicals as Roundup and specializing in producing food containing genetically modified organisms (GMOs). So Bayer is now positioned as a major player in the adulteration of the foods and chemicals that enter millions of human bodies worldwide. In her online article "Monsanto-Bayer—Two Destructive Corporate Conglomerates Become One," Maryam Henein says, "How convenient. They can make us sick with their poisonous, genetically modified faux food, and then treat us with their treadmill of drugs. [This] consolidation will create supply-chain dominance, aka vertical integration, in a $100 billion global market." Thus a single German corporation has the unique power to help implement the human enslavement agenda of the Reptilians by the manipulation of human biochemistry in billions of the worldwide population!

MEDIA AND MIND CONTROL

Of high importance to this system is control of all the public media. Keeping employees in the dark depends on what they read or view in their spare time. The masses can be made to believe that they have freedom of expression, but in reality it is the managers at the top levels of the media who decide what to feed the minds of the populace and so to keep them engaged and working in their corporate roles. Furthermore, this arrangement is supported by the psychological and psychiatric establishments in the major twentieth-century industrial countries, especially Germany and the United States. By imposing a form of public operant conditioning, which is the control of social stimuli, they obtain the desired responses. This is really akin to hypnotic suggestion, which becomes a type of populace mind control, which is the ultimate Reptilian goal. In its extreme form, it can result in Pavlovian conditioning, which is a more mindless and automatic form of conditioning. This is really a semi-hypnotic system in which a knee-jerk reaction to some sort of unrelated stimulus is elicited. This was portrayed in the 1962 film *The Manchurian Candidate* (remade in 2004), in which the "candidate," upon hearing a few numbers or a code word over the phone from his "controller," embarked on a plan to murder an important politician. Both types of conditioning are forms of mind control, or MK-ULTRA. This will be covered in chapters 13 and 14.

PART 3

THE FOURTH REICH
UNDER THE ICE

9

Nazis on the Moon and Mars

From all indications, the Nazi-Reptilian alliance began in the 1920s, long before Hitler came to power. Hitler was introduced to the aliens by means of his friendship with occultist Dietrich Eckart, who was a member of the Thule Society. Eckart invited Hitler to the black magic séances of the society because his astral contacts had identified Hitler as the incarnation of the Antichrist and the leader-to-be of the new Germany that Eckart had fervently been seeking. In my book *Alien World Order,* I say, "In those sexual black magic sessions over the three-year period from 1920 to 1923, there is evidence that Hitler's personality changed as he became taken over by a powerful malevolent entity. Eckart believed that it was the Antichrist." Eckart had no way of knowing or understanding that his astral contacts were actually Reptilians. The Reptilians are known to inhabit the Fourth Dimension and to masquerade as demons to impress the gullible occultists. They could not reveal themselves as aliens because that idea was much too far outside the comprehension of these eager-beaver demon seekers. So it could be said that Hitler became demonic, but in reality he became taken over by those masters of the astral realm, the mentally powerful Reptilian overlords. Once he was taken over, the Reptilians controlled Hitler and paved the way for him to create a dictatorship and for Germany to abandon democratic rule. The Reptilians always prefer to deal with one individual idea to bring about their political agenda, in this case, fascism. This was a radical transformation for Germany. Even Otto von Bismarck, the "Iron Chancellor" of the nineteenth century, had to defer to democratic principles, although he thoroughly dominated the German Empire. But this was the first time that an uneducated commoner like Hitler with absolutely no political experience or royal pretensions had taken over complete control of Germany, and it was really the Reptilians that made it happen. On his own, there was absolutely no way for Hitler, someone of such mediocre intellect and talent, to have effected such a grandiose achievement.

A REPTILIAN REICH

For the next ten years, from 1923 to 1933, important financial and political connections were made for Hitler by the Reptilians. These were connections that the ex-corporal could not have ever made for himself. He lived a charmed life, just as he had in World War I. His famous book, *Mein Kampf,* was written for him by Karl Haushofer. Even the title was not his. Finally, in 1933, he found himself as chancellor of Germany and his Nazi Party came into control of the German government. With the burning of the Reichstag and the passage of the Enabling Act of 1933, Hitler became a modern-day Caesar, and like Caesar, he insisted on being hailed in obeisance by the populace. It was during this ten-year period that the Nazis were made aware of the Reptilian base under two miles of ice on Antarctica. It also was revealed to them that this was to be their new home, that they would eventually join their Reptilian compatriots in Antarctica and would then be given space-faring science and technology, while Germany itself would be reduced to ashes. This was known because the Reptilians were in possession of a Chronovisor, a device for viewing probable future events. As early as 1943, when the American army landed on Anzio Beach in Italy, Hitler knew that the war in Europe was lost, and it was then that he had Martin Bormann build him a new home at Inalco, near Bariloche, in Argentina.

Once having placed him in power, the Reptilians paved the way for a fascist takeover of the planet. This was their ultimate plan, although they never expected to win this war. They had "other fish to fry." First and foremost, Hitler needed an army. In 1933, Germany was under the strict control of the Treaty of Versailles to limit their armed forces to one hundred thousand men for all military units combined. All they really had were a lot of dispirited, aging veterans of World War I and young, inexperienced draftees. The Reptilian scientists had a history of cloning biotechnology stretching back thousands of years in Draco, their home world. It was not difficult for them to produce a cloned army of one million fighting men of just the right age in their underground laboratories and on their space ships. Based on what I have learned from ex-supersoldier Penny Bradley (see chapter 16), I would venture to say that these men were probably cyborgs, since thousands of cyborgs have been produced on Mars for the Mars Defense Force (MDF) (see chapter 12) and the slave trade, and they were trained to just obey orders. Bradley is a veteran pilot of the Dark Fleet, now living here on Earth, who went through the Nazi Twenty-and-Back program, and has now, in her sixties, recovered all her memories of that experience.

And so it was that in September 1934, on the vast parade grounds of Nuremberg, Hitler gazed out at 160,000 of his newly minted legions, all properly armed with rifles and backpacks and standing at attention, their helmets glistening in the sunlight. Then came the advanced weaponry, the so-called wonder weapons, including rockets, jet aircraft, and huge submarines capable of crossing the Atlantic underwater. And finally they developed a totally new science and technology—antigravity propulsion. Flying discs would have been the ultimate weapon and by themselves would have won the war, but they came too late.

THE ANTARCTIC EXPEDITION

However, the ending had been foreseen by the Reptilians. They knew that once American industries came up to speed none of the wonder weapons would matter and that Hitler, like Napoleon and the kaiser before him, could never hope to win a two-front war. They also realized that a cloned army, no matter how large, could never defeat an army of creative-thinking individual soldiers, each of whom could devise strategies for every situation, whereas the robotic German troops could only follow orders, no matter how ill conceived. And so when the tide of war began to turn in 1943, the German generals realized they must prepare for the end. But the Reptilians already knew the ending, and so they had begun their preparations a year before the war began! In 1938, they persuaded the Nazis to mount a massive exploration and settlement of Antarctica. Such a complicated and expensive operation had to be at the behest of the Reptilians. It seems impossible that a nation contemplating what they knew would result in a world war would have begun such a vast exploratory operation six thousand miles away across the Atlantic Ocean, only one year prior to their invasion of Poland. Hitler knew that England would declare war immediately because of their defense compact with Poland. This suggests that the Antarctic project was actually of more importance to the Nazis than the war itself! And yet, they had no idea what they would find in that frozen wasteland! In his book *Germany's Antarctic Claim: Secret Nazi Polar Expeditions,* Christof Friedrich says, "There were no sources at that time which could provide even the barest hint of what was to be discovered, for as late as 1930, merely 15 percent of Antarctica had been explored, and that only tentatively by hardy trekkers who were mainly concerned with their own immediate problems of survival. In all of recorded history, fewer than 400 people had been to the continent!"

Make no mistake, this was an expensive project, at a time when Germany had only recently escaped from such crushing inflation that it took a wheelbarrow full of reichsmarks to buy a loaf of bread. But now, in 1938, they could afford expensive, sophisticated armaments as well as settlement of the Antarctic. The expedition was directed by Hermann Göring, second in command only to Hitler. But it also was known to involve the mysterious Thule Society, of which Eckart had been a member. In *Germany's Antarctic Claim,* we learn that "the following top-level government bodies were directly responsible for the proper outfitting of the research vessel and the planes: The German Naval High Command: The German Air Force High Command: The Reichs Finance Ministry: The Reichs Ministry for Food and Agriculture: Lufthansa, the German national airline: The Norddeutsche Lloyd Shipping Company, a quasi-government steamship company: The Deutsche Werft, Hamburg, a shipyard engaged in top-secret naval construction including submarines and surface vessels." This was a cross section of the entire German financial, military, and industrial superstructure. This mission was obviously very important to the future of both the nation and the Nazi Party.

THE VOYAGE OF THE *SCHWABENLAND*

Everything about this operation was first class and meticulously planned. The ship itself, the *Schwabenland,* was perfect for the ice-filled Antarctic waters, even though it would be sailing during the Antarctic summer. It carried two catapult-launched seaplanes and a trove of electronic monitoring equipment—very advanced for that era. In *Germany's Antarctic Claim,* we learn that "the scientists, experts and their assistants, were carefully selected from the sponsoring government bodies, as well as universities and research institutes. Far from being flabby, bespectacled ivory tower types, these men of the mind were selected for their physical fitness, as well as their academic achievements. Rarely in the history of exploration has there been such interdisciplinary co-operation and cross-fertilization in politics, philosophy, science, diplomacy, and all branches of government, including the military." The captain, Alfred Ritscher, was a legendary Arctic explorer who, twenty-five years earlier, had been forced to abandon his icebound ship in Arctic waters and walk for seven days over ice floes before getting rescued, losing fingers and toes to frostbite. Critical in this company were the agriculturists, revealing the expedition intentions of developing a colony with a self-sustaining food supply.

The mission was cloaked in secrecy. All the participants were segregated by their area of expertise. Strict military security was followed. According to *Germany's Antarctic Claim,* "All technicians, scientists and crew members worked on the 'need to know' principle. This principle was carried to the extent that those concerned with the compilation of scientific data: the airmen, technicians, oceanographers, biologists, meteorologists, etc., had their own quarters and ate in a mess room separate from the ordinary crew members." The book also tells us, "To compound the mystery, the ship took on board a great number of sturdy, tightly-sealed crates and boxes, which fell under the personal control of Doctor Todt, who was officially the Secretary of the Expedition. As these often heavy containers were not entered on the ship's cargo manifest, unsuspecting crew members asked Doctor Todt what their contents might be. In answer to their questions, Todt was as silent as death." Fritz Todt was a loyal member of the Nazi Party and, in 1938, was Hitler's minister of armaments. It makes sense that, in that capacity, he would know what was in those containers and also that they probably had to do with the antigravity flying disc propulsion technology (see plates 6 and 7).

NEUSCHWABENLAND

The explorers knew exactly what they were looking for. They carved out a large chunk of Queen Maud Land bordering the Weddell Sea and named it Neuschwabenland. They dropped fifty weighted four-by-six-foot swastika-flagged pinions all over that territory from the seaplanes, believing that it now belonged to Nazi Germany. However, that claim was denied in 1952, when all of Antarctica became an international zone by sanction of the United Nations, permitting foreign colonies but no annexation of territory. In that area, the Nazi explorers discovered large ice-free areas and warm-water lakes, which they named the Rainbow Lakes because of the color of the algae, and also found deep crevasses crossing the continent from north to south. When they descended into the crevasses, they were amazed to see that they widened into huge caverns. They also uncovered a deep freshwater trench under the ice cover from the north shore to the south through the area of Neuschwabenland. This under-ice waterway provided perfect access to the caverns, giving submarines warm-weather debarkation points, and they found a tunnel running from the Weddell Sea to those landing points. By the time the Antarctic winter set in, the expedition had, with the help of their Reptilian friends, identified a viable protected area in the caverns in which to locate their colony. And very likely, that is where they unloaded their secret cargo.

THE FÜHRER'S SHANGRI-LA

As the Wehrmacht rolled over Europe, the buildup of the Antarctic base continued at a frenetic pace. The demands of the war had no effect on the burgeoning colony, both in terms of personnel and construction projects as well as scientific and industrial development. Following that initial incursion, the Nazis sent out numerous exploratory missions to the Queen Maud region from South Africa, which had a white supremacist government at that time. Altogether, about 360,000 square miles were mapped from the air, which became Neuschwabenland. This base was in the Muhlig-Hofmann Mountains, very close to the Princess Astrid Coast.

The Omega File is a remarkable, comprehensive exposure of all of the secret international operations and events that have transpired in the twentieth century, written by Bruce Alan DeWalton, now deceased, who adopted the nom de plume of "Branton." Just as with the Ascension Glossary (qv), it exists only online.

According to the Omega File, "Various scientific teams were moved into the area including hunters, trappers, collectors and zoologists, botanists, agriculturists, plant specialists, mycologists, parasitologists, marine biologists, ornithologists, and many others. Numerous divisions of the German government were involved in the top secret project." An article in *Plain Truth* magazine in the United States in June 1952 said, "In 1940, the Nazis started to amass tractors, planes, sledges, gliders, and all sorts of machinery and materials in the south polar regions . . . for the next four years Nazi technicians built, on Antarctica, the Führer's Shangri-La. . . . They scooped out an entire mountain, built a new refuge completely camouflaged—a magic mountain hideaway." According to the Omega File, "One vast ice cave within the glacier was reportedly found to extend 30 miles to a large geothermal lake deep below." The Nazi engineers constructed buildings in the colony that could withstand temperatures of −60 degrees Fahrenheit. The entire colony was built in the massive caverns two miles beneath the ice, with easy access by submarine through the tunnel from the Weddell Sea.

NEU BERLIN*: A CITY UNDER ICE

By mid-1943, as the tide of war changed, the Allies noticed increased submarine traffic in the South Atlantic. At that point, the Neuschwabenland development project was taken out of the control of Hermann Göring and turned over to Heinrich Himmler. Therefore, it now became an SS operation. Göring's reputation had plummeted after he lost the Battle of Britain, and the British fighters and bombers were now wreaking major damage. Also, the British army was back in the fight after the miraculous rescue at Dunkirk. So the renewed attention to Neuschwabenland probably reflected the new wartime reality, with Himmler now focused on making Neuschwabenland a racially pure Aryan colony. He selected 10,000 young Ukrainian women, all blonde and blue-eyed, and 2,500 battle-hardened Waffen SS soldiers

---

*German spelling

to breed the new race to become the foundation of the Fourth Reich under the ice in the now burgeoning city of Neu Berlin. The buildup of Neuschwabenland was massive. According to noted Third Reich researcher and writer Rob Arndt, "After the war the Allies were able to determine that fifty-four U-boats were missing from Nazi Germany." He says also that "between 142,000 and 250,000 people were unaccounted for, including the entire SS Technical Branch, the entire Vril and Thule Gesellschafts, 6,000 scientists and technicians, and tens of thousands of slave laborers." This also included the so-called Lost Battalion. The SS Technical Branch was under the direction of Himmler and was the group responsible for the development and manufacture of the antigravity discs. Clearly, they all ended up in Antarctica. This explains how the Nazis were able to defeat Admiral Richard E. Byrd's armada in Operation Highjump in 1946 (see plate 8). It has been estimated that the current population of Neu Berlin is two million.

Fig. 9.1. Nazi manual for Neu Berlin

HIMMLER'S ANTARCTIC SPACE PORT

Himmler was a rabid believer in occultism, and in his sinister SS castle in Wewelsburg, he conducted séances to contact the demons in the astral realm, who we now know were really Reptilians. So it was probably through Himmler that contact and coordination with the Reptilians continued. Since we know that the Reptilians had an ancient colony in Antarctica, it is reasonable to conclude that they convinced him to become involved in the Neuschwabenland project after Göring's status declined and he lost interest. But more importantly, Himmler was made to understand that winning the war was no longer the long-term Nazi objective. It was the postwar situation that mattered, and the future of the Nazi party was no longer confined to Earth. It was now in the solar system, and beyond. It is not clear how the Reptilians were able to expand Himmler's horizons, but we do know that he eagerly adopted his new role as a galactic leader of the Nazi Party and the coordinator of the transformation of Antarctica into a spaceport. Apparently, the Reptilians liked the idea of a ruthless, amoral human contingent doing all their earthly dirty work for them, especially humans who enjoyed enslaving and abusing large masses of people and using them for genetic experimentation. As we have learned in previous chapters, the Nazis fulfilled that role perfectly. Also, they acted as cold-blooded intermediaries in obtaining human flesh and blood for the Reptilians. It was a marriage made in hell. And so this cosmic partnership was forged, and these soulless humans got to continue their jackbooted Nazi authority off the Earth as long as their Reptilian overlords found them useful.

Himmler had many clashes with Albert Speer, who became the minister of armaments after the death of Todt in a plane crash in 1942, and he blatantly attempted to bypass Speer and go directly to Hitler to take over all matters related to armaments. Speer describes all these conflicts with Himmler in his book *Infiltration: How Heinrich Himmler Schemed to Build an SS Industrial Empire,* published in 1981. Himmler delighted in using concentration camp inmates as slave labor. To him, they were simply disposable, whereas Speer wanted to treat them all with dignity and respect, including the Jews, and give them technical jobs, allowing them to live with their families. As Himmler took over more and more of the armaments manufacturing, Speer relied on his influence with Hitler to oppose him. But that influence began to wane as Hitler became mesmerized by Himmler's seeming grasp of the amazing new technology and his management of the Antarctic colony. Also, Hitler knew of the postwar plans for the Nazi Party, whereas Speer was kept in the dark. And Hitler knew that he himself would survive in Argentina. Speer says on page 230 of his book, "As the war advanced, Himmler interfered more and more insolently with the affairs of my ministry. Usually he turned to [Hans] Kammler with regard to large-scale construction projects churned out by his brain, which was indefatigably preoccupied with new ideas." Speer, of course, did not know about Himmler's responsibility to the Neuschwabenland colony, so he could not assess why Himmler did what he did. Also, he knew nothing of the top-secret antigravity technology development, which was under the direction of SS General Hans Kammler at the massive Skoda Works munitions plant near Pilsen, Czechoslovakia. Kammler, a civil engineer, was highly regarded by Himmler because he had designed and built the Auschwitz concentration camp, including the Zyklon B poison gas delivery component.

OPERATION TABARIN

In late 1945, after the conclusion of the war, in what became known as Operation Tabarin, British commandos from the secret Maudheim Base in Antarctica discovered the entrance to the tunnel leading to the Nazi base under the Antarctic ice shelf in Queen Maud Land. According to an article in the August 2005 issue of *Nexus* magazine by British historian James Roberts, the soldiers "followed the tunnel for miles, and eventually came to a vast underground cavern that was abnormally warm; some of the scientists believed that it was warmed geothermally. In the huge cavern were underground lakes; however, the mystery deepened, as the cavern was lit artificially. . . . The Nazis had constructed a huge base into the caverns and had even built docks for U-boats, and one was identified supposedly. Still, the deeper they traveled, the more strange visions they were greeted with." They ultimately discovered "hangars for strange planes and excavations galore." Only one commando survived that operation. He told his story to a new team, which took up Operation Tabarin II in October 1945. They were more successful, blowing up the entrance to the tunnel. One surviving team member from that heroic group said, "As we looked over the entire cavern network, we were overwhelmed by the number of personnel scurrying about like ants, but what was impressive was the huge constructions that were being built. From what we were witnessing, the Nazis, it appeared, had been on Antarctica a long time."

We now know that the "strange planes" were antigravity discs because the very next year Byrd's fleet, which was sent to destroy the Nazi base, was greeted by flying discs that came out of the water and destroyed at least two American ships and killed sixty-eight U.S. Marines. This was the failed Operation Highjump, a defeat that brought about the end of Byrd's military career. Himmler didn't live to see this triumph. He had already committed suicide to avoid being taken captive by the Russians.

THE NAZI FLYING SAUCERS

The German antigravity disc technology advanced rapidly after the project was taken away from Göring and turned over to Himmler in 1943. Himmler gave the project to Kammler and removed it from Germany to the Skoda Works in Czechoslovakia. Kammler's group built three working models of the now-famous Haunebu type. In my book *Secret Journey to Planet Serpo,* I say, "This was the distinctive bell-shaped craft powered by the rather simple electro-gravitation motor called the Kohler converter, developed by Captain Hans Kohler based on the

Tesla coil. This motor converted the Earth's gravitational energy into electromagnetic power, but could also extract energy from the ambient vacuum in outer space. In this series the Haunebu I was a small, two-man ship, but the Haunebu II was much larger and more sophisticated. It was reported to have a diameter of about seventy-five feet and had the capacity to carry a full crew." I say further in my book, "The German S.S. plans for this craft, dated November 7, 1943, are available on the internet. Also available are photos of the Haunebu in flight, clearly showing the German cross painted on the side and flanges, and a 75 mm antitank gun mounted on a swivel turret, apparently identical to the gun being used on German Panzer tanks."

U.S. General George S. Patton's Third Army arrived at the Skoda Works in mid-April 1945, six days before the Russians. By that time, there was no evidence of the Haunebu development and manufacture and Kammler was gone. He was never found. Clearly, he had escaped to Neuschwabenland by plane and submarine, along with the plans and models of the Haunebu. So his expertise became available to the Antarctic scientists around that time, which helps to explain why the Nazis were ready for Operation Highjump in late 1946. Evidently, the discs had been perfected during 1946, so they were ready for action by the next Antarctic summer, when the Byrd operation began.

Fig.9.2. SS General Hans Kammler mysteriously disappeared in 1945.

FIRST SPACE VOYAGES

The noted Bulgarian-born researcher and self-described "dissident scientist" Vladimir Terziski claims that a different antigravity propulsion technology was used for the so-called Vril craft designed by the German scientists Richard Miethe and Rudolf Schriever. These discs were developed in the early 1940s. According to Terziski, "The Miethe rocket craft was built in diameters of 15 and 50 meters, and the Schriever-Walter turbine powered craft was designed as an interplanetary exploration vehicle." He claims that it was this technology that achieved a moon landing as early as 1942. He says, "First landing on the moon by the Germans was at Mare Imbrium on August 23, 1942, at 11:26 MEZ, using a Miethe rocket. . . . The first man on the Moon was Kapitanleutnant Werner Theisenberg of the Kriegsmarine. Landing took place without radio contact to the main control center at the Wilhelmshaven or the second control center located near Anzio, Italy. Ever since their first day of landing on the Moon, the Germans started boring and tunneling under the surface and by the end of the war there was a small Nazi research base on the Moon." This mission undoubtedly originated somewhere in Germany. However, after the war, all Nazi space travel originated from Neuschwabenland. This was given the code name Base 211.

Fig. 9.3. Bulgarian researcher and self-described "dissident scientist" Vladimir Terziski

10

Base 211

The Nazi plan to implement the Fourth Reich depended on the take-over of the American economy, especially banking, as well as the media, the aerospace industry, and the military. They never expected to win World War II once the United States entered the war in 1941, despite Hitler's public bluster to the contrary. All of his speeches had only one purpose—they were all calculated to win over and maintain the worship and trust of the populace, and it worked. But the military leaders knew better. They knew that America was a "sleeping giant," protected from invasion by two oceans, with tremendous industrial potential, and that they wouldn't be able to compete with America's industrial might once it was set in motion. They had learned well the lesson of the kaiser. Chief of Staff General Ludwig Beck refused to swear an oath of loyalty to Hitler for that reason and resigned in 1938. Even during the war, they had depended on American-built Ford vehicles, as well as refined American petroleum. However, they knew that they would be ahead in terms of new bioscience and aerospace technology and weaponry once it was moved to Antarctica, which would allow them to take the upper hand in the solar system, especially on the moon and Mars. So they basically abandoned their European base of power and focused on building a base of operations in South America and Antarctica as early as 1943. This may also explain why they decided to invade Russia instead of England and America. They wanted to keep the American industrial superstructure and economy intact until they could take it over. They were supremely confident because they had the Reptilian technology and a solar-system-accessible base of operations in Antarctica to rely on.

The Reptilians had many reasons for wanting human colonies under their control out in the solar system and beyond. But mainly their plan was to get their Nazi lieutenants there first so that they would be in control when the rest of the human race achieved space travel and settlements and the humans could then be enslaved to work on other planets, as they were on Earth. When the "Star Trek generation" would arrive on the moon and Mars, they would encounter perhaps toned-down versions of Auschwitz, where "Work Makes One Free" would be emblazoned over the entrance gate and where slavery could be used because the human spirit would be crushed. And that is the current situation. The only humans who are now permitted to come to Mars are slaves, unless they are part of the Interplanetary Corporate Conglomerate (ICC; see chapter 13) or the MDF (see chapter 16). Base 211 was the key to the Nazis' expansion out into the solar system. Even though they were developing facilities all over Argentina, their main technical and scientific assets were concentrated in Antarctica.

We know that the Nazis had plenty of aboveground space as part of Base 211. It may be recalled that in the first expedition of the *Schwabenland* in 1938, they discovered large ice-free areas. It is very likely that they constructed spaceship launch facilities in those areas, where they had easy access of men and materials from underground. Most likely these were camouflaged to prevent detection from above (see plate 9).

HANS KAMMLER

In 1944, Himmler convinced Hitler to put the V-2 rocket project directly under SS control, and on August 8, Kammler replaced Walter Dornberger as its director. Kammler, a civil engineer who had made his reputation by planning Auschwitz, with its gas chambers and its human

*Fig. 10.1. SS General
Hans Kammler*

ovens, had a special talent for building huge underground facilities, employing slave labor, and getting projects done on time. But he also understood complicated engineering details and was uniquely capable of supervising advanced scientific programs. It was for this reason that Himmler had put him in charge of the antigravity project at the Skoda Works, where the Haunebu craft was being built. So Kammler became the most knowledgeable person in Germany about antigravity spaceship design.

From January 31, 1945, Kammler became head of all missile operations at Peenemünde, Germany. This meant that Wernher von Braun, the German pioneer in rocket technology, now answered to Kammler. Kammler thus became partially responsible for the V-2 bombardments of London. The Allied armies were now in France and advancing rapidly toward Berlin. But Hitler ordered that the V-2 facility remain in place until the moment the war front reached Germany's borders. Kammler was promoted by Himmler to the top rank of the SS, and he was now the fourth most important person in the Third Reich. But he was now stretched very thin since he also remained responsible for the entire secret antigravity weapons program at the Skoda Works. Hitler had realized that his only hope for winning the war was to defend against Allied bombing by getting the Haunebu militarily effective, which was why he depended on Kammler. But time had run out, and he was now planning his own survival.

KAMMLER AT BASE 211

In March 1945, partially under the advice of Goebbels, Hitler gradually stripped Göring of several powers on aircraft support as well as maintenance and supply while transferring them to Kammler. This culminated in the beginning of April with Kammler being raised to "Füehrer's general plenipotentiary for jet aircraft." Since the last V-2 on the western front had been launched in late March, on April 1, 1945, Kammler ordered the evacuation of five hundred missile technicians to the Alps. On April 5, Kammler was charged by the Oberkommando of the Army to command the defense of the area around the city of Nordhausen. However, rather than defend these missile construction works, he immediately ordered the destruction of all the "special V-1 equipment" at the Syke storage site to keep this top-secret facility out of enemy hands. That was Kammler's last known act. He then disappeared and never again reappeared.

Kammler's disappearance was a great disappointment to U.S. General Dwight D. Eisenhower, the supreme commander of the Allied Expeditionary Forces in Europe. Four different versions of his "death" were being circulated, all of them involving some form of suicide. We now know that Kammler remained very much alive and that he and his team had escaped to Base 211. When there, he was instrumental in the rapid development of the Haunebu craft in Antarctica. And this explains the flight of the Haunebu III to Mars in 1945 and the defeat of the American forces in Operation Highjump in 1947. As previously mentioned, thousands of slaves had already been sent to Antarctica by Himmler on large capacity so-called "milk cow" submarines, as well as a contingent of six thousand German scientists, so Kammler's workforce was already in place.

NEW BERLIN

Base 211 was really part of a much larger colony in Antarctica that was not settled by Germans. It was connected to a city coincidentally called New Berlin, which apparently was much older than Base 211 and originally had no relationship to Berlin, Germany. A strange book titled *Base: New Berlin,* written in German, was recently sent, unsolicited, to Kerry Cassidy at the Project Camelot website. It was written by someone named Barabou Vedu. He claims that he lived in that city for several years in a "huge building of glass and plastic, several square kilometers in area." He claimed that people on the base spoke English and an "Indian" language, although he himself spoke German. It is believed to have been an ancient extraterrestrial colony inhabited by diverse alien groups speaking languages that the author believed to be "Indian." Apparently, the Nazis used this colony as the foundation for Base 211. Vladimir Terziski (see chapter 9) claims that New Berlin is now a modern city of over two million inhabitants. Apparently, it now has tall office buildings and industrial areas able to accommodate contemporary corporate offices and manufacturing facilities. In all probability, the Nazis were "given" this facility by their Reptilian friends, but they have now built it into an interplanetary base, although author Jim Marrs said the extraterrestrial quarter still exists and is inhabited by a diverse group of aliens living peacefully alongside their Nazi neighbors.

As New Berlin expanded, advanced scientific research and industrial capacity grew quickly. This attracted the interest of existing German aerospace manufacturers who had started operations prior to, or had survived, the war and were now drawn to the Antarctic colony. Michael Salla, in his 2018 book *Antarctica's Hidden History,* says, "In early 1939, the German secret societies had decided that their space program would relocate to Antarctica, whose remoteness and deep cavern system under two miles of ice, accessible only by submarines, would provide all that was necessary to build such a program without possible disruption from the impending war" (see plate 10). Salla says further in his book:

During World War II, extensive submarine activity in the region of Antarctica indicated that the Nazis were building more bases, in addition to the one Captain Ritscher's expedition had established [in 1938]. U.S. Navy spies reported that once it became possible, major German companies involved in the Nazi's military-industrial complex began moving equipment, resources, and personnel down to Antarctica, using Nazi Germany's vast fleet of submarines, according to William Tompkins. Companies such as I. G. Farben, Krupp, Siemens, Messerschmitt, United Steelworks, etc., were just some of the many involved in the Antarctica operations which Tompkins specifically recalls from the Navy spies intel.

Such advanced companies as Luftva Aeronautics, which was involved in advanced flight propulsion systems and space station design, Astro und Feinwerktechnik Adlershof GmbH, a manufacturer of attitude control components and supplier of space systems, and DSI GmbH, Jena-Optronik, and Daimler AG were just a few of the companies involved. Funds for the rapid expansion of Base 211 were readily available from Argentina, where Bormann was sitting on top of mountains of money from German banks as well as precious metals, the "loot of conquered Europe." When Hitler arrived in Argentina, in late 1945, it is possible that he directed Bormann to divert huge investments to the development of Base 211.

NAZI INFILTRATION

Meanwhile, things were swiftly changing in postwar America. The Nazi takeover of the United States began with Operation Paperclip. In my book *Alien World Order,* I say, "At least 1,600 scientific and research specialists and thousands of their dependents were brought to the United States under Operation Paperclip. Hundreds of others arrived under two other Paperclip-related projects and went to work for universities, defense contractors, and CIA fronts. The Paperclip operation eventually became such a juggernaut that in 1956 an American ambassador characterized it as 'a continuing U.S. recruitment program that has no parallel in any other Allied country.' The Nazis had learned well the art and science of fifth-column infiltration from their Reptilian overlords, whose ancestors had destroyed and sunk beneath the waves the entire continent of Atlantis, home of the most advanced civilization ever to appear on this planet.

Eventually, ex-Nazi scientists and technicians came to play a dominant role in the American aerospace industries and as contractors in the American military. This dominance reached a crescendo in 1960 with the appointment of Wernher von Braun as the director of the Marshall Space Flight Center in Huntsville, Alabama, the central facility of NASA. Now, an ex-Nazi SS officer who had been instrumental in the V-2 rocket bombardment of London, killing thousands, sat in the top position of America's burgeoning space program. The Nazi takeover of the American aerospace industry was now complete.

As the Nazi scientists became integrated into American aerospace corporations, these companies became "Germanized" and took on an international aspect, rather than American, especially as the people running them became impressed with Nazi technology. Thus, as the fifties progressed and as the executives at these companies secretly became aware that Nazi scientists were sending missions to the moon and Mars, they were anxious to open facilities at Base 211. Eventually, New Berlin became an international high-tech enclave of sophisticated space technology, much like Silicon Valley today. Most major American aerospace companies and scientific facilities became represented at Base 211.

THE EISENHOWER MEETING

Eisenhower, by this time the U.S. president rather than a general, met with an alien contingent at Holloman Air Force Base near Alamogordo, New Mexico, in February 1955 and made an agreement with them. There is plenty of evidence for this meeting. However,

Eisenhower believed the aliens to be from elsewhere in the galaxy, whereas they were actually Reptilians from underground bases on Earth. The agreement permitted the aliens to abduct humans on a limited basis, with full reporting back to our government, in exchange for advanced technology. As they always do, the Reptilians broke the agreement almost immediately and began large-scale abductions without reporting. The abductees were used to create hybrids and for forced labor at Base 211 and on the moon and Mars. Many abductees were enslaved and traded to other extraterrestrial civilizations. Members of the U.S. military were abducted, exposed to advanced technology, and trained as supersoldiers. They became instrumental in the alien Milabs program and were used to advance the alien agenda in the United States and on the moon and Mars.

THE U.S. TAKEOVER

While the Nazis infiltrated and began to dominate the aerospace industries in the 1950s, at the same time, they moved into our government and intelligence agencies and removed anyone who stood in their way, as was the case with President John F. Kennedy. Clearly, it was no accident that both of the Dulles brothers, John Foster and Allen, came into national public office in 1953, one year after Eisenhower began his presidency. In my book, *Alien World Order,* I say:

> General Eisenhower's move into the presidency in 1952 brought into power the ultraconservative Republicans who before and after the war had business and banking connections with Nazi Germany and who had been in sympathy with many aspects of the Nazi philosophy. John Foster Dulles became Secretary of State, and his younger brother, Allen Dulles became the director of the CIA in 1953. These two canny veterans of insider Washington skirmishes now had, between them, a lock on American foreign policy and a powerful influence on domestic policy. They were easily able to

Fig. 10.2. CIA Director Allen Dulles

manipulate the naïve, but well-intentioned president, who had absolutely no political experience.

The history of the Dulles brothers' affiliation with Hitler went back twenty years to his ascension to power in 1933. As lawyers with Sullivan and Cromwell in New York, representing the Kuhn, Loeb Company, they met with Hitler in Cologne, Germany, on January 4, 1933, to negotiate short-term financing for Hitler to run for chancellor of Germany. Later, both brothers were founding members of the Council on Foreign Relations, whose avowed goal was one-world government, the so-called New World Order. In *Alien World Order,* I say, "The ex-Nazis who were infiltrating the U.S. government all sought to advance this globalist agenda. It was covertly understood by the deep insiders that this was really a code phrase for the Fourth Reich."

Over at the CIA, Allen Dulles had developed a friendship with Reinhard Gehlen, the ex-Nazi spymaster who now directed the Gehlen Org, a CIA asset in Germany that employed almost exclusively ex-Nazi spies. Again, in *Alien World Order,* I say, "Given Dulles's history displaying sympathy for Nazi causes, it seems reasonable to conclude that Allen Dulles brought many of the Gehlen Org agents into the CIA. In fact, in those early CIA days, the entire organization was dedicated to anti-Soviet activity and to 'fighting' the cold war. Consequently, virtually all of the spies that Gehlen had employed in Europe were brought en masse to constitute the entire early CIA organization." Their Nazi histories were scrubbed from their records.

THE EISENHOWER SPEECH

When Eisenhower came to the end of his presidency in 1960 and turned it over to Kennedy, he delivered a farewell speech that clearly implied that he understood what had happened during his eight years in office. Having met with the aliens in 1955 and now having a retrospective view of what the Dulles brothers had wrought, he felt that it was his patriotic duty to enunciate a dire warning to the American people. Eisenhower was obviously cognizant of the serious inference of the speech since it went through twenty-one drafts. He began by helping us to comprehend the huge implications of our new situation when he said:

> Now this conjunction of an immense military establishment and a large arms industry is new in the American experience. The total influence—economic, political, even spiritual—is felt in every city, every statehouse, every office of the Federal government. We recognize the imperative need for this development. Yet, we must not fail to comprehend its grave implications. Our toil, resources, and livelihood are all involved. So is the very structure of our society.

This is a remarkable statement. It is a recognition that the military has now assumed tremendous importance in American life independent of any military challenges from other countries. Those with ears will understand that what he is saying is that the danger is now from within. From this, one should logically ask the question, "How can our military be such a danger and threat to the American populace whom those in its ranks are sworn to defend, and how can it threaten 'the very structure of our society'?" He was implying that some dangerous

*Fig. 10.3. President Dwight D. Eisenhower and rocket scientist
Wernher von Braun with aerospace engineers*

foreign element had crept into the U.S. military establishment. He was referring here to the Nazi influence.

If that is true, it explains fully the rest of the speech and why it took twenty-one drafts to get his point across diplomatically, choosing his words very carefully. He went on to say, "In the councils of government, we must guard against the acquisition of unwarranted influence, whether sought or unsought, by the military-industrial complex. The potential for the disastrous rise of misplaced power exists and will persist." The only reason that Eisenhower, an ex-general who knew well and trusted the military, would warn America about a possible military coup was the possibility that it could occur because of that Nazi influence. In other words, he knew that the Nazis had worked their way into the very fabric of our military-industrial complex. And as evidence of that, even as he gave that speech, Wernher von Braun was taking over the desk of the director of the Marshall Space Flight Center at NASA.

Fig. 10.4. Wernher von Braun with Saturn V rocket engines

A DARK PARTNERSHIP

Following the Eisenhower speech, active cooperation between the Nazis and the American military-industrial complex began in earnest. Salla says in *Antarctica's Hidden History:*

> The Dulles brothers, [Prescott] Bush, and U.S. bankers, industrialists, and public officials made it possible for a confluence of U.S. and German companies to reach agreements that would establish the Fourth Reich and the U.S. military-industrial complex as partners. Within a strictly compartmentalized security system, large

U.S. companies worked with their smaller but more senior "German partners" in expanding out the industrial facilities in Antarctica. However the U.S. companies were often left in the dark about the full details of how their products would be used. The final result of this system was that fleets of antigravity spacecraft were built in Antarctica under full German control; not only for interplanetary colonization, but also interstellar conquest alongside their Reptilian/Draconian partners. Certainly, that meant that was also the birth of the U.S. space program. Both [Bill] Tompkins and [Corey] Goode have described the threat this "Dark Fleet" posed for different human-looking extraterrestrial civilizations.

So, ironically, it seems that the birth of the Dark Fleet in Antarctica, which was ultimately to be headquartered on the moon, had the full assistance of U.S. corporations. But, even more ominously, it was also the birth of the ICC, which was eventually to settle on Mars (see plate 18) and, ultimately, together with their Nazi Dark Fleet brothers, to rule the solar system with an iron hand.

11

Moon Bases

THE LUNAR OPERATIONS COMMAND

After that first moon landing in 1942, the Nazi base expanded rapidly, first beneath the surface and then above ground as they continued to send heavy construction equipment to the moon throughout the war in successive trips from Base 211 in Antarctica (Neuschwabenland), using the Haunebu I and II spacecraft. Initially, they were careful to minimize and disguise the surface evidence of the base, which was inside a crater, even though it was on the dark side, since they knew that even though the dark side was not visible from Earth, eventually there would be spacecraft from the United States and perhaps other nations orbiting overhead. But as that first colony expanded, they abandoned their concerns about discovery and constructed a large surface building complex in the shape of a swastika! Eventually, by the 1960s, it became an eleven-level, bell-shaped underground facility.

There were already existing moon bases established by alien groups, some of which were extremely ancient (see below). In an article published on May 20, 2015, on the Exonews website and on his own website, ExoPolitics.org, at a later date, Salla relates the testimony of Corey Goode, who was taken to the moon by Milabs operatives (see page 186). The Milabs agents were attached to that segment of the U.S. military that was working jointly with the Reptilians, the Grays, and the

Illuminati. This was the so-called Cabal. They had advanced propulsion technology and free access to the Nazi moon base, which ultimately became known as the Lunar Operations Command, or LOC. Even though it was under Nazi control, this base evolved into a sort of intergalactic United Nations type of facility, where representatives from throughout the galaxy could meet with entities in this solar system for commercial and/or political reasons. As will be seen, the Nazis from Base 211 in Antarctica became the Dark Fleet.

Salla says, "Corey describes the Moon as a neutral space used by various secret space programs and extraterrestrial civilizations that have established 'Embassy Zones.' He describes the Moon as very similar to Antarctica that is used by multiple nations that abide by international treaties for its peaceful use even though some nations may be enemies. Significantly, Corey's description of the moon as a diplomatic zone used by multiple space programs and extraterrestrial races matches another secret space program [described by] whistleblower Randy Cramer (who refers to himself as 'Captain Kaye' because he does still have that rank in the Marines), who had revealed what was happening on the Moon in an April 2014 interview." In that interview, Cramer says essentially the same thing: "It's kind of like Antarctica, it has these different areas where different countries and people can say we got this area, and we got this, and everybody respects everybody's claim or area. . . . Whether people are friendly or hostile, it's kind of a neutral territory, so there are places where those who don't get along with others [are] not too far from each other. But they don't attack each other [because] the

Fig. 11.1. Ex-supersoldier Randy Cramer, also known as "Captain Kaye"

contracts, [i.e.] diplomatic arrangements, [are] for that." Cramer claims that he had been part of a supersoldier contingent on Mars for seventeen years as an inductee in the Twenty-and-Back Program, in which an abductee serves twenty years in a military unit or other duties on Mars and then is mind-wiped, de-aged, and returned back to his or her normal life at the exact time he or she was initially kidnapped.

THE DARK FLEET BASE

One of the questions posed to Goode via email and reported in that same article on ExoPolitcs.org was:

Q: What can you tell us about the other shared human moon base used by the dark fleet?

GOODE: It is a heavily guarded and secret base that is at about the 10 o'clock position, on the back side of the Moon. The portion that is visible is a "Trapezoid Shape." It is only accessible to the Dark Fleet and some ICC Personnel as well as the Draco Allied Forces. Some amateur astronomers have caught videos of swarms of craft leaving from this base location on a couple of occasions. It is presumed to go far beneath the surface of the Moon just as the LOC does.

I was able to obtain considerably more information about this top-secret base from a mysterious source titled "Moon and Mars Bases" that was posted on the internet without attribution. It is uncertain how reliable this information may be, but the huge amount of detail testifies to its authenticity. From this article, we learn that there are five linked bases, mainly on the dark side of the moon, but protruding onto the left fringe as viewed from Earth, where there is still some available light, and therefore these bases are somewhat visible. However, apparently the aliens and Nazis did not feel it necessary to construct these bases underground. Actually, in view of the bases' purpose, that would have been very difficult, if not impossible, anyway. Because of the linkages, these bases actually compose a large single compound, which is the home base and headquarters of the Dark Fleet in this solar system (see plates 11 and 12).

Base #1 is an interstellar spaceport that accommodates large spaceships of different types from all over the solar system and beyond. Apparently, they have the ability to house and perform maintenance on a variety of craft. The above-mentioned article says, "Purpose: To Receive Space Ships of Different Kinds." This means that from here they also take off. Here ships get prepared for longer trips, same as in our international airports. They can land easily, so big ships prefer to come here to load or unload, then from this place they go down to Earth. A rather big area is in use with storage space included. Some very advanced technology is available on this base for installation and implementation of equipment on the spaceships that they service. They apparently have the capability of tailoring their technology to many different types of spacecraft. This base also includes a training facility to prepare the spaceship crews for various missions on different planets, including, especially, missions to Mars and Andromeda. This preparation includes the use of a cryogenic facility to fast-freeze bodies for long journeys. There are surface-level living quarters on the base for crews that must spend time waiting there for technology implementations or repairs or for training. The personnel on this base are not afraid of being observed from Earth since, superficially at least, it all seems peaceful from afar. The staff on this base consists of 199 ETs and 500 hybrids. They have the use of seventeen spaceships for administrative purposes. The base is surrounded by "half-vegetation" supplied with water from 1,500 feet under the surface.

Base #2 might be called the abductee debriefing station. This base is for higher-level abductees who will have considerable influence over others back on Earth and who therefore require more targeted and carefully designed debriefings. Highly trained "spies" attend debriefings and float around trying to elicit information that is not otherwise revealed. If "traitors" are discovered, they are shot. The abductees then go through a memory-erasure procedure. These missions are so secret that even the Gray workers going back to Andromeda go through this memory wipe. New arrivals are given data implants accompanied by special drugs. These implants remain in place under the level of the subconscious, which causes the implantees to act robotically. Humans who also go through this procedure are left with no memory whatsoever of having been to the moon, although they may experience unexplained pains, nausea, and dizziness. Secrecy and prevention of leaks is an obsession on this base. All information is recorded and double-checked. The staff consists of three hundred ETs, four hundred hybrids, and forty humans, all highly trained to play various roles and to stage scenarios to implant and discover information. These interrogation practices are highly reminiscent of what we know about Gestapo tactics, which connects this system to past Nazi operations on Earth. The staff members have fast ships at their disposal, which are needed for the abduction operations. The author of this report says, "Everyone seems free to go and do whatever he wants, while, in reality, they are all prisoners in different degrees. Real freedom is nonexistent; it is all a false appearance!"

Base # 3 is reminiscent of the Holodeck in *Star Trek*. It is dedicated to recreation. The author says, "Spaces have been created for different activities such as sports, movies, paths for walking, which at the same time link the different Bases . . . Machines for entertainment—Comfortable sitting spaces—Areas for sleeping—Swimming Pool—Small Stadium for contests—Machines for keeping it all in shape. Personnel in charge: ET's 30, as managers—150 hybrids for keeping the area."

Base #4 is the special coordination center. It is the smallest of the five bases in area and is the most important. It is the main Dark Fleet base on the moon. This base has the highest security and is considered a restricted area. The only work done here relates to very special missions and important people, especially the handling of "delicate" situations. From this base, communication lines radiate out to Earth, Mars, spaceships throughout the solar system and beyond, various other locations, and bases on other planets, especially those in Andromeda, which is their home galaxy, where all the ETs based here were trained. The working staff here consists of 100 ETs and 130 hybrids, who are very bright and highly specialized. *Homo sapiens* (i.e., humans) are expressly forbidden on this base, and if any are discovered, they are terminated. Any human who mistakenly finds himself or herself here will not leave alive. The entire base is protected by a special metal shield that is impervious to cosmic rays, and the base houses miniaturized computers with voluminous capacity, from which data of interest can be extracted and displayed. It is a very busy place, and the work done here is continuous, without a break. Tremendous electrical power is produced from small devices.

Base #5 is part of the same area as Base #4. All the energy for the entire compound is produced here. It houses the main workshop, where electromagnetic tools and lasers are used to repair mechanical equipment. The staff consists of 70 extraterrestrial engineers and 110 skilled hybrids. *Homo sapiens* are not permitted to learn these skills. Humans may watch these procedures, but they are not taught how to perform them. Since this is not a restricted area, the path made to come here is used for walking. There is no danger of radiation. It's unfortunate that *Homo sapiens* are not taught how the aliens produce energy here because it's a thousand times simpler than on Earth.

HUGE BABIES

British author Timothy Good says in his book *Above Top Secret*, regarding the Apollo 11 mission, "According to a former NASA employee Otto Binder, unnamed radio hams with their own VHF receiving facilities that bypassed NASA's broadcasting outlets picked up the following exchange:

NASA: What's there? Mission Control calling Apollo 11 . . .

Apollo: These "Babies" are huge, sir! Enormous! OH MY GOD! You wouldn't believe it! I'm telling you there are other spacecraft out there, lined up on the far side of the crater edge! They're on the Moon watching us!

In 1979, Maurice Chatelain, former chief of NASA communications systems, confirmed that Armstrong had indeed reported seeing two UFOs on the rim of a crater. "The encounter was common knowledge in NASA," he revealed, "but nobody has talked about it until now." Soviet scientists were allegedly the first to confirm the incident. "According to our information, the encounter was reported immediately after the landing of the module," said Vladimir Azhazha, a physicist and professor of mathematics at Moscow State University. "Neil Armstrong relayed the message to Mission Control that two large, mysterious objects were watching them after having landed near the moon module. But his message was never heard by the public because NASA censored it."

According to another Soviet scientist, Aleksandr Kazantsev, "Buss [*sic*] Aldrin took color movie film of the UFOs from inside the module, and continued filming them after he and Armstrong went outside. Azhazha claims that the UFOs departed minutes after the astronauts came out on to the lunar surface. Maurice Chatelain also confirmed that Apollo 11's radio transmissions were interrupted on several occasions in order to hide the news from the public."

Fig. 11.2. Alien craft on the moon (Drawing by William Tompkins).
For information about Tompkins, see chapter 17.

MONA LISA ON THE MOON

Italian journalist and UFO researcher Luca Scantamburlo traveled to Rwanda, Africa, on May 25, 2007, to obtain an interview with ex-U.S. astronaut William Rutledge, the commander of the alleged Apollo 20 moon mission in August 1976, who was living there at the time. This mission, a top-secret joint American-Russian operation, originated at Vandenberg Air Force Base in California and received absolutely no publicity. Rutledge was seventy-six years old at the time of this interview and was recalling events that had taken place forty-one years earlier, so some slips or gaps of memory are understandable. Nevertheless, his recall of dates, technical details, and events from so long ago was exceptional. Rutledge wrote the following in the foreword to the published interview: "I don't use English since 1990 but Kinyarwanda and French, and I write quickly, sometimes letters are missing because I'm busy writing the next one, or it is another on the keyboard, which is used, but that's a detail. . . ."

The sensational aspect of that mission was the investigation of a massive, extremely ancient alien spaceship that had been found completely intact and nestled in between two huge rock outcroppings on the dark side of the moon and which was first photographed by the crew of the Apollo 15 spacecraft from overhead. It was measured by the astronauts and found to be 11,056 feet long!

Fig. 11.3. The ancient alien spaceship found on the moon, compared in size with a New York City multiblock area

Figure 11.3 compares the craft to a New York City multiblock area. Inside was a smaller triangular craft. Nearby were the ruins of an ancient alien city with lofty spires. Two bodies were found inside the smaller craft, including, lying on her back in one of the pilot chairs, a perfectly preserved female (see plates 13 and 14). She closely resembled an ethnic Mongolian woman from Earth in terms of both facial features and complexion. Rutledge reported the discovery back to Mission Control at Vandenberg, at which time she was christened by one of the astronauts as "Mona Lisa," perhaps because of the perfection of her preservation, comparing that perfection to the painting by Da Vinci. Rutledge reported to Mission Control that the Mona Lisa "seemed not dead not alive." The other body, a male, presumably the copilot of the small craft, was in a state of serious deterioration, except for the head. The astronauts severed the head and took it back to the lunar module along with the intact Mona Lisa. Rutledge estimated the age of the spaceship to be about 1.5 million years old!

The following is an excerpt from the interview of Rutledge by Scantamburlo:

L.S.: What about the "Mona Lisa EBE" [extraterrestrial biological

Fig. 11.4. An image of the ancient spacecraft found on the moon

entity]? How does she look like and where was she at that time, when you found out her on the Moon. Where do you think she is now?

W.R.: Mona Lisa—I don't remember who named the girl, Leonov or me—was the intact EBE. Humanoid, female, 1.65 meter. Genitalized, haired, six fingers (we guess that mathematics are based on a dozen). Function: pilot, piloting device fixed to fingers and eyes, no clothes, we had to cut two cables connected to the nose. No nostril. Leonov unfixed the eyes device (you'll see that in the video) concretions of blood or bio liquid erupted and froze from the mouth, nose, eyes, and some parts of the body. Some parts of the body were in unusual good condition, (hair) and the skin was protected by a thin transparent protection layer. As we told to mission control, condition seemed not dead not alive. We had no medical background or experience, but Leonov and I used a test, we fixed our bio equipment on the EBE, and telemetry received by surgeon (Mission Control meds) was positive. That's another story. Some parts could be unbelievable now, I prefer [to] to tell the whole story when other videos will be online. This experience has been filmed in the LM [Lunar Module]. We found a second body, destroyed, we brought the head on board. Color of the skin was blue gray, a pastel blue. Skin had some strange details above the eyes and the front, a strap around the head, wearing no inscription. The "cockpit" was full of calligraphy and formed of long semi-hexagonal tubes. She is on Earth and she is not dead, but I prefer to post other videos before telling what happened after.

This remarkable discovery is clear evidence of ancient settlements on our moon. And we know now from the recent testimonies of Corey Goode and Randy Cramer that there are still many alien colonies on the moon, at least one of which possesses the huge craft that appeared on the rim of the crater during the Apollo 11 exploration. The claim that "she is not dead" is astounding! That an ancient civilization had the technology to preserve "human" bodies for over a *million years* stretches credibility to the breaking point.

MILABS MEMORIES

The returning memories of Milabs who were taken to the moon for short periods corroborate much of the information we have learned from other sources. In the article "Secret Moon Base Uses Abducted Humans as Slave Labor," published on his ExoPolitics.org website, Salla says, "A member of the public forum 'The One Truth' alerted Corey [Goode] to the claims of Carolyn Hamlett, who says that she witnessed a moon base that she was taken to. She recalled the shape of the base as being trapezoid and recreated it. Here is what she wrote about the re-creation."

> The picture is my creation from my memory. I put the picture together to illustrate what I have seen with physical eyes while aboard a lunar bound craft with other humans. The trapezoid shaped building was our destination. My first thought when I saw this structure was of its unique and significant shape, that of a de-capped pyramid and how much in architecture it reminded me of the Pentagon as seen in aerial photographs. Therefore, I chose a portion of an aerial photograph of the Pentagon to best illustrate the architecture of the actual building I saw on the moon. The rendition I have created is very much like the view I had as the craft I was in was making its approach. However, the actual building on the lunar surface does not have an inner court yard.

In an interview, Hamlett recalls being inside the spacecraft approaching the moon base she described in the above picture. She says that her memory then cut out in the craft, and she next recalled being inside the moon base and witnessed a council-type meeting with up to thirty global leaders from around the world led by a prominent female. She says that the base had been built in collaboration with Gray ETs who could not be trusted and were manipulating the humans at the base by misleading them into believing they were in control. Hamlett does not fully recall what happened during the rest of her time inside the moon base. [Update 5/25—In an earlier version of this article, I mistakenly wrote that Carolyn Hamlett had no memories of what occurred inside the moon base and described her trip as an abduction experience. In fact, she had partial recall of an event she experienced there, and writes it was not an abduction experience as she clarified in an update on her blogsite. I have updated the above article accordingly, and apologize to Carolyn Hamlett for the errors.]

According to Goode, there is very little intelligence on what is happening inside of the moon base used by the Dark Fleet [but see above]. In addition to Carolyn Hamlett's testimony, there is a Milab who claims to have been taken to a secret moon base where Gray ETs play a role, and recalls traumatic experiences happening to her.

Niara Terela Isley is a former U.S. Air Force radar tracking operator who was forcibly recruited into a covert program when she witnessed a UFO while performing her official air force duties when she traveled with other USAF personnel to an assignment at the Tonopah Test Range in 1980. She and her colleagues were instructed to attempt to get a radar lock on the glowing UFO, and were then taken into custody by a covert faction of the USAF. She was then exposed to a number of traumatic experiences in these MILABs that she describes at length in her book, *Facing the Shadow, Embracing the Light* (2013). She reveals that she was taken between eight and ten times to a secret moon base that was guarded by Reptilian beings and used human workers:

> In interviews, people always want to know what my moon experiences were like and I can certainly understand such avid curiosity. I can only state that it was terrible on multiple levels. I was terrified for my life the whole time. I was very poorly fed and worked hard during the day cycle, operating some kind of electronic equipment for excavation at times, and doing hard physical manual labor at oth-

ers, such as lifting and stacking boxes. Worst of all, I was used for sex during what passed for night there, from man to man. I was allowed very little sleep, and I've since learned that this is another facet of mind-control abuse. I shut down during all of this to the point that I didn't even feel alive anymore. (*Facing the Shadow, Embracing the Light*, p. 271)

Isley's description is testimonial evidence that slave labor is both used on the moon, and that milabs are taken there for that purpose either for short periods or for indefinite periods as occurs on Mars. While she did not describe the shape of the moon base she was taken to, her experiences with Reptilian guards and physical abuse along with other human workers suggests it is the Dark Fleet base that Goode has described. Furthermore, she described Gray ETs piloting the shuttle craft taking her to the moon, which is consistent with what Carolyn Hamlett said about the Grays being involved in the base's operations.

Goode's revelation of an exploitative "Dark Fleet" base on the far side of the moon is now supported to varying degrees by two independent witnesses (and tallies perfectly with what we already know about that base; see above). Hamlett's recollection of the base is that global leaders are taken there and manipulated by Gray ETs. Isley's recollection is that Grays and Reptilians are involved with at least one moon base, and allow human workers to be mistreated. Isley's testimony and the experiences of Carolyn Hamlett, when combined with Goode's revelations about secret space programs, leads to a disturbing conclusion. There is at least one secret base on the far side of the moon that manipulates human leaders taken there and uses abducted humans (Milabs) as slave labor.

A PAIR OF JEANS

John Lear has had a long and distinguished career as a commercial pilot and aviation authority. With that very pragmatic and scientific background, in which he was responsible for the lives of thousands of passengers on his planes, he would not be someone you would expect to entertain fantastic theories. However, Lear believes that the moon currently has a population of about 250 million human beings! And yet, when you see him defend that amazing theory in his YouTube videos, you very quickly become a believer also. Certainly, after reading the preceding material in this chapter, you would have good reason to believe him because it all points to agreement with the veracity of that belief, if not with the actual number of humans on the moon. That possibility becomes even more believable when Lear informs us that the gravity on the moon is about 69 percent of the gravity exerted on Earth and that the atmosphere is roughly equivalent to ours at an altitude of 18,000 feet, about the same as at the summit of Mt. Kilimanjaro. Lear says that it takes about one week of decompression to become accustomed to the thinner lunar atmosphere. The dissident scientist Vladimir Terziski agrees entirely. He says, "In my extensive research of dissident American theories about physical conditions on the Moon I have proved beyond a shadow of a doubt that there is atmosphere, water, and vegetation on the Moon, and that man does not need a space suit to walk on the Moon. A pair of jeans, a pullover, and sneakers are just about enough." This explains how such a large human population could exist on the moon.

The big question is: Where did all those people come from? Lear says they are not from Earth, by which I take it he means they are not from the Adamic race, which originated on Earth about fifty thousand years ago, as discussed in my previous book, *Alien World Order*. But they could have been descended from the Atlanteans, who were pre-Adamic. This would explain why they are far more spiritually advanced than we are.

In *Alien World Order*, I explained that the Atlanteans did not have the Reptilian brain since that was a genetic compromise that the Elohim agreed to when the Adamic race was created by the DNA from twelve other human races in this galaxy. This makes sense because we know that the Atlanteans had spacefaring technology and battled the Reptilians on the moon. It is perfectly understandable that a contingent of Atlantean fighters may have survived those wars and remained on the moon to found a moon-dwelling human race. As we now learn more about the subordinate condition of the humans on the moon, it appears that they may have become enslaved to the Reptilians, the dominant force on the moon, while on Earth they prevailed and forced the Reptilians to go underground. It is certainly possible that a small population of Atlantean humans could have grown to 250 million since the time of that ancient conflict about fifty thousand years ago.

12
Mars

THE FIRST TRIP

Vladimir Terziski is a Bulgarian-born engineer and physicist. He graduated cum laude from the master of science program at Tokai University in Tokyo in 1980. He served as a solar energy researcher at the Bulgarian Academy of Sciences before emigrating to the United States in 1984. Terziski is an international UFO researcher with a command of English, Japanese, Russian, German, and Bulgarian. He was the creator and lecturer of a Ufology 101 course for university-level attendance, probably at Tokai University in Tokyo, where he obtained his MS degree and became the president of the American Academy of Dissident Scientists.

In 1991, Terziski came into possession of a German documentary film created fifty years earlier that described the Nazi V-7 special weapons programs. The secret V-7 projects included circular aircraft research designs for the development of radical new weapons platforms that could rise and descend vertically and fly at supersonic speeds at very high altitudes using a new "implosion" motor design and other electrogravitic energy-conversion principles to produce a self-sufficient electrostatically generated force for power.

These engines were manufactured by Allgemeine Elektrizitäts Gesellschaft for this research program in 1944. Research along these lines had been carried out since 1941, earlier in the war. Allgemeine Elektrizitäts Gesellschaft was the great wartime electrical giant of industrial Germany at that time. These engines generated their own electro-gravitation field, which neutralized the Earth's natural gravity, in effect making them weightless. They were used to power the Haunebu anti-gravity discs, of which there were four models in the V-7 program, culminating in the largest model, the Haunebu IV. Allgemeine Elektrizitäts Gesellschaft also manufactured a different engine used for the smaller Vril models, of which there were seven. Then there was the mile-long cylindrical mothership carrier called the *Andromeda,* also antigravity, designed to transport the Haunebu and Vril craft in flight.

The first German trip to Mars originated in April 1945 from Germany itself and not from Base 211 in Antarctica. This may have been because they just didn't have the technological resources to launch such a complicated mission from Base 211 at that time. Another reason, perhaps, was because it was a joint German-Japanese mission and the Japanese were not willing, or able, to send their people across the now very dangerous waters of the South Atlantic in this last month of the European war. On the other hand, the facilities to launch such a mission might have been in remote areas of Germany untouched by Allied bombing, and the Japanese members of the crew had probably trained there and so were already stationed there anyway.

Terziski says that the craft used for the journey was a special, larger version of the Haunebu III sometimes referred to as the Haunebu IV. The chosen model was 74 meters, or 243 feet, in diameter, and could accommodate a crew of hundreds. It was powered by Andromeda tachyon* electro-magnetogravitic engines. It had three inverted gun

---

*The *Andromeda* craft is believed to have been the huge carrier craft over 100 feet in diameter designed to carry several Haunebu and Vril craft inside, like an aircraft carrier. Some say it only existed on the drawing board, but most likely the Andromeda-Gerat engine was designed for that craft, but was only used on the Mars mission on the expanded Haunebu III, which was a one-way trip. Tachyons are particles that travel faster than

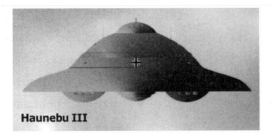

Fig. 12.1. The Haunebu III

turrets on the bottom and one on the top of the crew compartment. Early models of the Haunebu could not accommodate gun turrets because they interfered with the rotation of the craft, but evidently the engineers had solved that problem by 1945. Terziski claims that the large crew was necessary because electronic automation was still primitive at that time, and so all the controls had to be operated manually, as on a submarine. But the life-support operations were handled by small Kohler converters, which had been in use on the smaller Vril craft for several years.

Terziski says that an all-volunteer crew was necessary because it was considered a suicide mission, with a very low likelihood of returning to Earth. However, the Germans knew that there was a friendly indigenous Reptoid population on Mars that was available to help the cosmonauts, and probably Terziski did not have that information because it was highly classified. So, very likely, it was planned that the crew and passengers would remain on Mars to found a small human colony. That would explain why they sent so many passengers. There didn't seem to be any particular advantage, scientific or otherwise, to wasting millions of reichsmarks and sending hundreds of people to die on Mars! In fact, in all likelihood, one or more of the passengers may have been Reptilian to facilitate communications upon arrival. The Earth Reptilians and the Martian Reptoids are related and friendly, although the Reptoids are hostile to the Dracos.

(*cont. from p. 135*) light (i.e., superluminal). It is believed that tachyon engines have been developed in the Secret Space Program and that these superliminal craft are being used by the Nazis on Mars, and by the U.S. in the Solar Warden fleet. The engines were probably designed by German scientist Arnold Sommerfeld.

According to Terziski, the trip took eight months because after escaping from Earth's gravitational pull, they turned off the tachyon engines and basically coasted the rest of the way. He says that if they had continued under full power, the trip would only have taken two to three days. That seems hard to believe, but we really don't know anything about the tachyon engines. They would have had to be super-luminal. It is also possible that the ship went through a wormhole. They crash-landed on Mars and damaged the engines. So that made a return flight impossible anyway. But they were prepared to stay, and so the German Mars colony officially began in mid-January 1946.

ARIES PRIME

The colony grew rapidly through the forties and fifties, supplied with highly sophisticated construction equipment carried by Haunebu II craft. These trips originated from Base 211 and from Argentina. This fact alone debunks Terziski's belief that the Haunebu III journey was a suicide mission. By 1975, the colony had become a huge facility known as Aries Prime, about 90 percent of which was underground. This name is very appropriate since Mars is the astrological ruler of Aries. The Germans are very much into astrology. The Aries Prime facility incorporates some amazing technology, and it has become the "Grand Central Station" of the German presence on Mars. It now consists of three separate bases that are connected underground.

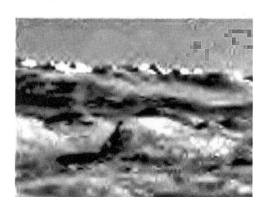

Fig. 12.2. A city on Mars

Base #1 is mainly used for receiving food and medicine supplies and storing spare parts for the spaceships. Most of the spare parts are used on Earth at Base 211, and the food comes mainly from Earth. This has promoted heavy traffic between Earth and Mars, possibly even daily trips. It is a massive facility and can accommodate huge interstellar and intergalactic ships in a protected underground facility. Ships constantly come and go, and sometimes there may be up to three ships docked there at one time. This base has twenty spaceships of its own. As of the late nineties, there were about 100 humans, 350 hybrids, and 30 ETs living and working there. The official language is Standard High German, although other dialects are tolerated. Since there is heavy trade and commercial activity there from all over the galaxy, the base has a hospitality function and is designed to welcome and accommodate visitors from across the galaxy and to provide tours of the facility. However, there are strict classified levels, and a need-to-know basis prevails. There is underground water, so they can grow food there using hydroponics, and they can keep and propagate a large animal population. There is a hospital there with a psychiatric ward that uses very advanced psionic technology, including the ability to implant and remove memories! This keeps everyone in line and reduces any possibility of a revolt. As everywhere under German/Nazi control, large slave populations are used and must be kept pacified. And even the working staff must also be kept under control. There is no real freedom at any German facility in the solar system!

Base #2 is the nerve center of the facility. This is where worldwide information is gathered, coordinated, and applied to situations as they develop. It might be said that this is the combined CIA/FBI of the entire German operation on Mars. Consequently, it supercedes the moon operation, and directions and orders for the LOC originate here. Needless to say, this is very high tech, so this is where the smartest people are found. As of the late nineties, there were 400 ETs, 3,000 hybrids, and 500 humans employed at this base.

Base #3 is a combined educational and training center. Orders are sent out from here, usually through the Mars internet, which is used for computer face-to-face sessions. Some training and implantation takes place onsite, while in other cases, trainers and instructors travel to bases on Earth and the moon. These people have to think and react quickly since plans change rapidly. The staff consists of 350 Greys, 300 hybrids, and 75 humans. These trainers have their own ships and sixty of the best pilots assigned to them. Humans are not permitted to fly these ships since the Nazi officers are afraid they might escape from Mars.

As can be seen from this, Aries Prime has to be massive to accommodate all these people and craft. It would be easily seen from Earth, either by orbiting craft or through telescopes, but most of the activity is underground with only a small visible presence in a crater. But there are many other smaller bases all over Mars.

THE AMERICAN MARS EXPEDITION

The first U.S. mission to Mars landed on the Martian surface on May 22, 1962. Amazingly, a video of that landing exists and can be viewed online! See that video here: https://youtu.be/ydgIMV-1EBE. It was supposedly unmanned, but the view out of the window of the spacecraft and the accompanying comments and cheers by the crew and their surprised exclamations when they see some small creatures burrowing into the Martian soil definitely seem to be coming from onboard the craft, although they could possibly have been coming through an intercom from Base 211. But that would mean that the view of Mars through the spacecraft window was being televised and sent in real time to the war room at Base 211 and that the personnel there were responding with cheers, also in real time, and that all this was being recorded on tape in the craft—a highly unlikely technical scenario in 1962. So everything points to the conclusion that it was a manned mission.

This was a top-secret mission that has not been referenced in any NASA documentation to our knowledge. It would have remained top secret if this video had not been downloaded recently. Actually, the information that there were small burrowing creatures on the surface of Mars was confirmed in 2018 via a comment by the ex-supersoldier Captain Randy Cramer, who says that he spent seventeen years on Mars, in one of his public talks. As far as we know, that was the first time this phenomenon was ever mentioned.

WERNHER VON BRAUN AND MARS

Superficially, at least, there doesn't appear to be any involvement of Wernher von Braun in this mission to Mars. On the date of the landing, May 22, 1962, which was mentioned in the video, von Braun had only recently, in 1960, become the director of the Marshall Space Flight Center, the central facility of NASA, in Huntsville, Alabama, and he was immediately caught up in Kennedy's determination to put a man on the moon in seven years. After coming to the United States in 1945 as part of Operation Paperclip, he, along with his German Paperclip rocket team, had been initially confined to the U.S. Army base at Fort Bliss, Texas. While there, unable to leave the base without a military escort, he instructed military and scientific personnel in the principles of rocketry while his team worked on rehabilitating V-2 rockets shipped from Germany and testing them at the nearby White Sands Missile Range in New Mexico. He remained at Fort Bliss for about five years, until 1950. But strangely, it was while he was there that he wrote his book *Das Marsprojekt* (*The Mars Project*) which was published in German in 1952. All the science, mathematics, and technology for a mission to Mars was laid out in that book.

This was seven years after the German aerospace scientists in Antarctica had already succeeded in sending a manned mission to Mars. It's unlikely that von Braun had any role in that 1945 mission. He had just recently arrived in the United States and was confined to Fort Bliss. And it's very likely that the 1962 mission used the Haunebu III or IV, which was probably launched from Base 211. They just didn't have the rocket power for the trip at that early date, whereas von Braun's book

Fig. 12.3. Wernher von Braun's book Das Marsprojekt

was based entirely on the use of rocketry. They would have needed the heavy lifting of the Saturn V, and that wasn't ready until 1967. His book describes a very impractical plan for a rocket trip to and from Mars. Furthermore, we now know that a joint United States–Soviet Union mission was sent to Mars in 1964 and that a base was established there. Von Braun appeared to be out of that loop too. In the preface to the English-language edition of his book, he speculated that a workable round trip to Mars would not be possible until 1977.

In retrospect, it seems highly unlikely that the rocket engineers and scientists in Antarctica didn't know that Germany's preeminent rocket scientist was on American soil in Texas, especially since they were now consorting with American aerospace engineers at Base 211. I think that the Nazi plan was to allow von Braun to go through the Paperclip processing to give them influence with the U.S. space program while somehow staying in touch with him. If there was indeed a line of communication between them, then that might explain von Braun's book. And that would explain why it was written in German. It means they probably helped him write the book in order to impress his American associates.

AN AMERICAN HAUNEBU

But then, as a director of NASA beginning in 1960, von Braun was in a position to secretly plan and monitor an American mission himself, by now being fully informed about the Haunebu and antigravity technology by his Antarctic associates. The U.S. moon landing was still seven years in the future, and the Saturn V rocket, first used in 1967, did not yet exist. This means the U.S. scientists would have had to use much less powerful rocketry for the Mars mission. Without the heavy-lifting capability of the Saturn V, it is doubtful that they could ever reach Mars with a human crew in any acceptable time frame. The mission might take about two years one-way. We don't know when they departed Earth, but even if it was in 1960, no rocket-powered space-ship existed that could make that trip, land safely on Mars, and return to Earth. That leaves only one inescapable conclusion: the American mission used a Haunebu III or Haunebu IV spacecraft and probably departed from Base 211 in 1961 or 1962. Von Braun may have possi-bly been involved in the planning. Since that mission has remained top secret, it has not been necessary to reveal the existence of antigravity spaceships.

This means that there was active cooperation between U.S. and German aerospace companies. But none of this is surprising now that we know about the German-American technical cooperation in Antarctica beginning in 1955. In 1950, at the outset of the Korean War, von Braun and his team were moved to the Redstone Arsenal in Huntsville, Alabama, where he became the director of development for the Army Ballistic Missile Agency. He could now travel freely to Argentina and Antarctica whenever he wished, so he may have played a consulting role in the 1962 mission.

Von Braun's main job at NASA now was to keep America's space program slowed down to a crawl, allowing only occasional triumphs like the moon landings, while real progress was being made at Base 211, where traffic throughout the solar system was proceeding at a lightning pace. Already, by the time he took over NASA in 1960, the LOC was well developed and the Mars bases were sending spaceships to the asteroids and the moons of Saturn. Human colonies already existed on Ceres, Phobos, and Titan. The Dark Fleet was now immersed in protecting and facilitating profitable mining operations at these places while operating from their headquarters on the dark side of the moon (see chapter 11), trading with a rapidly expanding extraterrestrial clientele and using a slave population derived from abductions on Earth.

THE DARK FLEET

As the space program at Base 211 in Antarctica developed in the forties and fifties, there were more and more secret missions to the moon and Mars for various purposes. Consequently, the bases in both places expanded correspondingly. The LOC became a very large facility, able to handle traffic from all over the galaxy, including to and from Mars and Earth. This growth was supervised and controlled by the Dark Fleet. From their base on the dark side of the moon (see chapter 11), they essentially became the police force for traffic in the solar system. They maintained a close working relationship with the Reptilians, who kept them supplied with the latest technology and weaponry. In fact, they accompanied and joined in Reptilian missions of conquest and exploitation, even beyond the solar system.

It is very likely that the Dark Fleet was initially staffed with ex-Nazi soldiers who came through the "ratlines" to Argentina and Antarctica on the large "milk cow" submarines. It is known that Himmler took steps to ensure that all of the immigrants to Antarctica were of pure Aryan descent, and consequently the German military was a major source of personnel, since they had all been genetically "checked out." These men constituted an Antarctic defense force, and it was almost certainly from these ranks that the Dark Fleet pilots were taken and trained. Almost all the abductees who had any contact with the Dark Fleet said they all had a Nazi aspect. Corey Goode says they all wore black uniforms and were severe in character and attitude and capable of killing or inflicting merciless treatment—all very reminiscent of the earthly Nazis who committed atrocities. In answer to a question from Michael Salla, Goode said, "It is true that the Dark Fleet personnel have been called 'Storm Troopers' and 'Space Nazis' both because of the way they act, dress, the symbols they wear as well as the shape of their Vessels (Star Wars like). They are very dark individuals who work alongside the Draco vessels mostly outside the Sol System helping them in offensive activities against enemies of the Draco Joint Federation."

PART 4

THE INTERPLANETARY
FOURTH REICH

13

The Interplanetary
Corporate Conglomerate

*The ongoing interaction between humans within the Deep
Black World of the Intelligence/Security apparatus and
the Aerospace community with non-human intelligences
has an occultic basis that was thousands if not millions of
years in the making. There is nothing new about humans
interacting with and working for non-humans.*

JAMES BARTLEY

After the successful 1962 mission to Mars and the establishment of the
joint United States–Soviet Union base in 1964, traffic increased from
Earth. Aries Prime wasn't yet founded, but German bases were begun all
over the planet in what appeared to be a connected and very organized
fashion, under some sort of central authority. This authority cannot be
identified, but it was clearly under Nazi control and could have been
the Bavarian Illuminati. Hitler's influence was fading, especially among
the German scientists and engineers, but Bormann was still very much
a Nazi. Now in Argentina and yielding financial control, Bormann was
taking over the leadership. Also, the Vatican was very much in the picture. At some point in the early sixties, with von Braun now installed

as the director of NASA, it was decided to relocate the entire corporate structure from Base 211 to Mars, which was a more suitable central location for the now busy traffic in the solar system. A skeletal corporate park remained in Antarctica, since the American aerospace corporations— although infiltrated by German scientists and technicians—had taken over what became known as the Secret Space Program. So because of the preponderance of American corporate employees, English became the language of choice, spoken across the board, and American culture now prevailed throughout Base 211. With von Braun at NASA and Kammler the chief military authority in Antarctica, the Germans, especially the Nazis, wanted their own German-speaking technology facility. Mars was, like the Old West, a lawless territory, and so offered the Germans a location for a scientific headquarters of their own. Since the Nazi-dominated Dark Fleet already controlled the moon through the LOC, a German technological center on Mars was needed to support their scientific operations. The new base on Mars was given the name of the Interplanetary Corporate Conglomerate, or the ICC. Most of the Base 211 corporations opened a facility at the ICC, and German became the official language. The ICC is now the Martian version of Silicon Valley, although vastly more advanced, especially in bioscience.

The main ICC base on Mars was constructed in the southern hemisphere by the companies participating in the base in Antarctica. Some of these were corporations intending to keep their main corporate facilities on Mars and some were contractors. Some of the main participants in building the first base were a mix of American and German corporations including TRW, North American, Philco, Lockheed Martin, Douglas Aircraft Company, General Dynamics, Northrop Grumman Space Technology, NASA, JPL Planetary Resources, Boeing, Astro- und Feinwerktechnik Adlershof GmbH, Advanced Space Technologies GmbH, and Jena-Optronik. Taken all together, they constituted the ICC.

All of this information is from Ileana, the Star Traveler, who worked with the ICC for fifty years and then was age-regressed back to her life on Earth as a teenager. She claims that it all comes from her memory, which is rather astounding! Ileana says, "These are the aerospace contractors that contributed to the various military bids to build out bases, as well as the orbital space platforms near Mars. . . . Some of these contractors are fully briefed on what exactly the work is that they do and other smaller contractors are on a need-to-know basis doing the work but not told where the manufactured parts go in space or to whom. There are permanent shareholder companies which contribute financial and technical support to the various ICC committees and councils." According to Ileana, the propulsion manufacturers are Ad Astra Rocket Company from the United States, which provides advanced plasma rocket propulsion technology; AE Aerospace, from the United Kingdom, which provides hybrid ion rocket engines; and Lutva Aeronautics from Germany, providing advanced flight propulsion systems and space station design. Ileana also delineates the spacecraft component manufacturers. See appendix A for a complete list of German/Nazi off-world technologies.

Major shareholder companies are Allianz (German), AmerisourceBergen (American), Aviva (British), Bayer AG (German), Biogen Inc. (American), Boeing (American), Daimler AG (German), Exxon Mobil (American), General Dynamics (American), Gilead Sciences (American), GlaxoSmithKline (British), JPMorgan Chase (American), Lockheed Martin (American), NASA JPL (American), Merck (American), Monsanto (American, now acquired by Bayer), Kroger (American), Pfizer (American), RAND Corporation (American), Siemens (German), Syngenta (Swiss), and Talanx (German). It is interesting to see the major pharmaceutical companies on this list, which suggests the importance of drugs in these ICC operations.

The ICC has constructed four large space station satellites around Mars, which were designed by von Braun (see plate 15). They house small human communities, and they are used to monitor all physical and communications traffic to and from the Red Planet. Allied with Dark Fleet warplanes, they also are used to keep out whoever the ICC pleases and to make sure that Mars remains a Teutonic planet.

THE FOURTH REICH

Thus the Fourth Reich came into existence. It was not only international but also now interplanetary! With the founding of Aries Prime in 1975 and the rapid advancement of the ICC in the eighties, Mars has now become a completely German planet and the home of the Fourth Reich. They have now made Aries Prime into a capital city, and their range has spread out to ten other smaller subordinate cities dotting the Martian landscape under their control. The Dark Fleet base on the moon became their version of the Pentagon. That base possesses awesome technology and weaponry, including nuclear, and an air force capable of destroying any opposition in the solar system, including the United States. Supported completely by their powerful allies, the Draco Reptilians, who have even more advanced technology, they roam the galaxy jointly conquering and controlling other civilizations. Together, with their nuclear weapons capability, they actually now have the capability of destroying a planet!

According to the ex-supersoldier Randy "Captain Kaye" Cramer (see plate 17), the Germans have a large military contingent quartered on Mars, possessing weaponry that is comparable to anything that can be found in sci-fi comic books! While preferring mainly Aryan/Nazi soldiers, they also have the ability to abduct selected individuals from any country on Earth and elsewhere to bolster their ranks and to train them as supersoldiers under the military command of Nazi officers. This has evolved into the MDF, which basically exists to protect the burgeoning Mars commercial operations and the ICC (see plate 18).

The German Martian pioneers had to deal with two indigenous populations. There was a Reptilian colony on Mars that was not connected with the Reptilians in Draco or those on Earth. Cramer calls them Reptoids, and after many years on Mars and after being held captive in their colony for six months, he developed an admiration of their culture. He said they were basically peaceful but could field a fierce fighting force. The native Reptoids view the Dracos as invaders and have fought battles with them in which the Reptoids have prevailed. There is also a race of so-called Insectoids on Mars. They resemble insects on Earth, having four arms, two with pincers, but are generally over six feet in height. They are highly intelligent, and they too are basically peaceful but are very organized militarily. These could have been the Ant People spoken of by the Hopis, who claim that they were helped by them in an underground colony in Arizona. Cramer says that the three colonies exist on Mars in a sort of military standoff posture, with occasional flare-ups. He also says that he was one of the few survivors of an underground confrontation between the MDF and the Reptoids, in which a thousand humans were killed.

CYBORGS

Ileana, born as Elena Kapulnik in the Ukraine in 1985, was abducted as a child and was taken to Mars. She now refers to herself as Ileana, the Star Traveler.

Only two years old when first abducted, she was trained as a lan-

Fig.13.1 Elena Kapulnik, aka Ileana, the Star Traveler

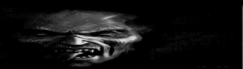

ARCHONS

HIDDEN RULERS THROUGH THE AGES

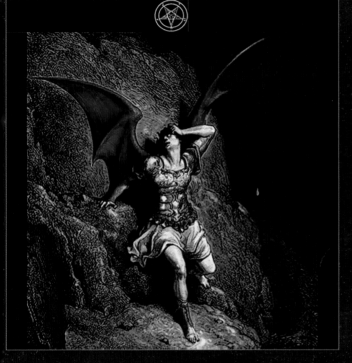

Plate 1. *The Archons*

Plate 2. *A Draco Reptilian*

Plate 4. *The sinking of the Lusitania,*
May 7, 1915

Plate 5. *A Nazi "pagan-reincarnation" parade*

USAF Top Secret Nuclear Powered Flying Triangle - The TR-3B

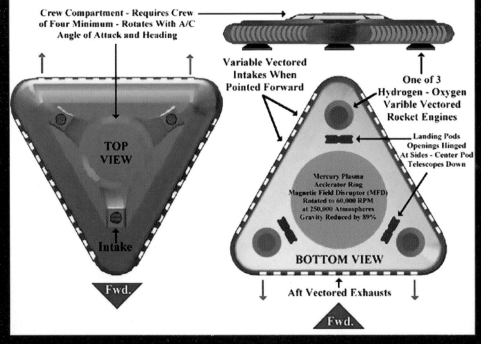

Crew Compartment - Requires Crew of Four Minimum - Rotates With A/C Angle of Attack and Heading

TOP VIEW

Intake

Fwd.

Variable Vectored Intakes When Pointed Forward

One of 3 Hydrogen - Oxygen Varible Vectored Rocket Engines

Landing Pods Openings Hinged At Sides - Center Pod Telescopes Down

Mercury Plasma Accelerator Ring Magnetic Field Disruptor (MFD) Rotated to 60,000 RPM at 250,000 Atmospheres Gravity Reduced by 89%

BOTTOM VIEW

Aft Vectored Exhausts

Fwd.

Plate 6. *An antigravity disc, known as the TR-3B*

Plate 7. *An antigravity disc in flight*

Plate 8. *Nazi antigravity discs attack U.S. Navy ships,*
Operation Highjump, 1946

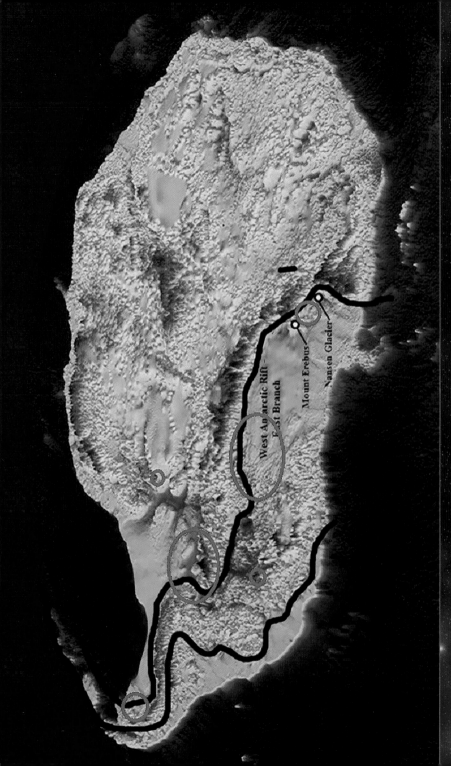

Plate 10. *Locations of "under-the-ice" industrial cities in Antarctica [red circles]*

West Antarctic Rift —
East Branch

Mount Erebus

Nansen Glacier

ALPHA

LUJAN ARCHIVOS OVNI

German moon base / base lunar alemana

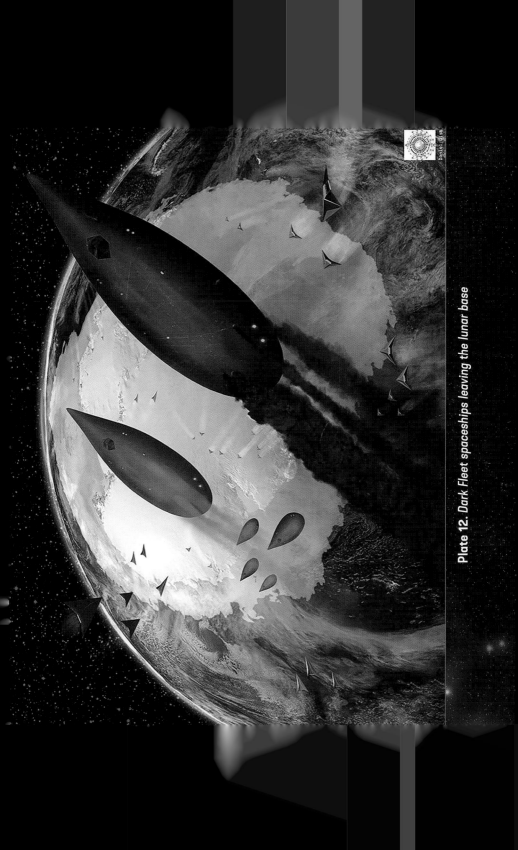

Plate 12. *Dark Fleet spaceships leaving the lunar base*

Plate 13. *Preserved body of female alien pilot, dubbed "Mona Lisa," discovered on the moon by Apollo 20 crew*

Plate 14. *Artist's re-creation of the "Mona Lisa" alien pilot as she might have looked in life*

Plate 15. *One of Wernher von Braun's Mars satellites*

Plate 16. *A German railway cannon*

Plate 17. *Randy "Captain Kaye" Cramer on Mars*

Plate 18. *Remote ICC Base on Mars*

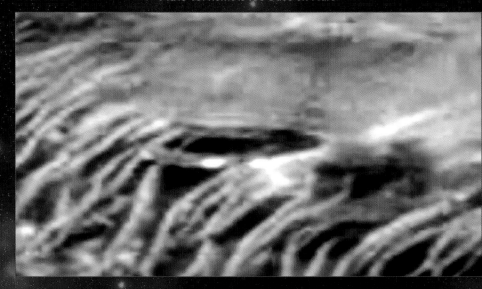

Plate 19. The Ride of the Valkyries *by William T. Maud, 1890*

Plate 20. *Ad for William Tompkins's book* Selected by Extraterrestrials

Plate 21. *Wernher von Braun with President John F. Kennedy, 1963*

Plate 22. *Solar Warden secret space program*

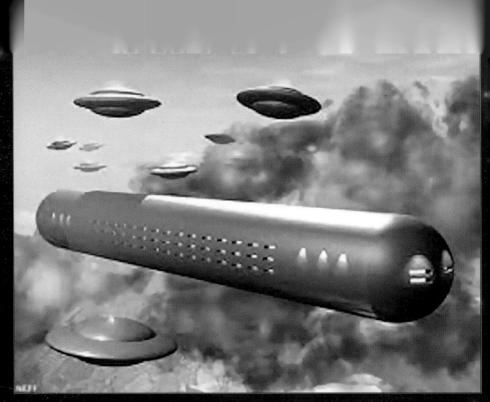

Plate 23. *Solar Warden spaceship*

Plate 24. *A nuclear submarine bed, New London, Connecticut*

guage specialist to ultimately act in the role of a translator of the bewildering diversity of human and extraterrestrial languages represented on Mars. Recently age-regressed back to a teenager and returned to Earth, she is now speaking out as she remembers her experiences on Mars. She now has near-total recall of her sixty years working for the ICC. As she has slowly recovered her memories, she has learned a lot about herself. (See appendix A for an explanation of how this works.) For instance, when her father started visiting a gun shop and bringing home weapons, she discovered that she could handle knives and axes and was a sharpshooter with a pistol and rifle. These are not skills that suburban teenage girls normally pick up by reading instructions! (To understand how all this works, see the "Age Regression" section in chapter 15, on page 156.) She claims that the ICC has grown to a massive size and has become the dominant force in the solar system. Now supported by the Dark Fleet, it controls all extraterrestrial traffic in and out of the Mars airspace. It is an amazing testament to the efficacy of the German Martian genetic testing laboratories to have identified Ileana's potential language capability at the age of two so that they could build on that ability through special training. We have learned from some of the other abductees that somehow the German scientists have access to the soul records of abductees and so can tell what they will be capable of as adults. This must have some involvement with the Akashic Records.

Ileana spent almost all of her time on Mars working in the Cybernetics Laboratory, which is part of the ICC, and she now speaks of the astounding feats that laboratory was able to accomplish. The main work of the Cybernetics Laboratory is the creation of cyborgs. These are humans who have been modified by the integration of psionic and electronic physical and neurological implants in their bodies and brains to create supersoldiers who become virtual robotic slaves. She says that the ICC has developed a very lucrative trade in cyborgs throughout the galaxy! They are a very valuable commodity for civilizations trying to develop instant armed forces. Corey Goode says that the ICC trades with over nine hundred extraterrestrial civilizations. Needless to say, the German scientists have no concern for any suffering the human soul in a cyborg body might experience. They are, after all, Nazis.

Ileana says that multiple cyborgs can be created to look identical. Or they can be given any designer physical characteristics that the scientists choose. They also can be made to look identical to a living person in every detail, including eye color, the shape of the nose, hair color, voice, height, and weight! This is done through nanotechnology.

NANOTECHNOLOGY

Ileana says that the scientists at the Cybernetics Laboratory are now using nanotechnology extensively. Nanotechnology was originally conceived by American physicist Richard Feynman in 1959 at the California Institute of Technology, popularly known as CalTech, but it could not be put into practice, given the science of that time. It involves conducting science and technology applications in nanometers, which permits the direct manipulation of atoms and molecules. One nanometer is a billionth of a meter, so there are 25,400,000 nanometers in one inch. In 1970, Professor Norio Taniguchi of the Tokyo University of Technology coined the term *nanotechnology,* and then the advent of the scanning tunneling microscope in 1981 and later the atomic force microscope made it possible to use nanotechology for scientific applications. It is this technology that makes it possible to achieve such fine distinctions in cyborg technology. Ileana says its usage was developed by the German scientists at the ICC by reverse engineering extraterrestrial technology. It has obvious application in intelligence operations.

SOUL TRANSFERS

According to Ileana, the ICC Cybernetics Laboratory has the ability to remove the soul from the body and then store it temporarily in an electromagnetic stasis chamber or transfer it to another body. Memory engrams can also be removed and stored on microchips and then implanted in another body, which can be a clone or another human. These can be short-term or long-term memories. Usually, the recipient would be "mind-wiped" or "blank-slated" before receiving the new engrams. But in some cases, the new memories can overlay the recipient's existing memories, which the recipient comes to believe are his or her own. The engrams can also be transferred from the microchips to a computer cloud on a satellite and then downloaded later from digital format to biological format. I discussed this technology in my book *Alien World Order,* in which I revealed information shared by Robert Morning Sky, a Native American who learned it from his grandfather, who got it from an extraterrestrial survivor of a pre-Roswell UFO crash in New Mexico. He claimed that the bioscientists for the Reptilian queens of Orion have had this capability for thousands of years. Consequently, it seems highly likely that the German scientists learned this technique from their Reptilian friends.

REGEN TANKS, RESURRECTION, AND LIFE EXTENSION

The ICC scientists and physicians are routinely using medical techniques that are considered miraculous here on Earth! Cramer claims he has lost limbs in battle that were restored in a "regeneration tank" in a matter of days, sometimes hours. These tanks literally regrow the missing limb! Cramer says his foot was bitten off by an Insectoid soldier to prevent him from walking, but he was rescued and the foot was restored in a hospital. He says his limbs have been restored several times over the course of his seventeen-year enlistment. Others, including Penny Bradley and James Rink, have also spoken of the "regen tanks."

Christian biblical scholars will be astounded to learn that resurrection of the dead is also a common procedure on Mars. It can only be employed under certain ideal conditions, but it works by dialing certain settings in a regen tank. Bradley claims that she initially took comfort in the knowledge that she could escape from intolerable situations by allowing herself to be killed. But after being returned to full consciousness several times, she finally realized that death was not the answer. So she resigned herself to just following orders, became numb to her situation, and reluctantly remained alive. The ICC also cheats death in another way. They have developed life-extension biotechnology and can keep humans alive past the age of one hundred. I also discussed this phenomenon in my book *Alien World Order* as another scientific breakthrough developed by the scientists of Orion, many eons ago.

SMART SUITS

We also learn from Ileana that the ICC scientists have developed so-called smart suits. They protect the wearer from bullets and electromagnetic directed-energy weapons. Nanotechnology is built into the suits so that, when the suit is turned on, the wearer can amplify his or her agility and running speed, walk through walls, levitate, communicate with computers, and create invisibility through a cloaking device. A food and nutrient supply is built-in, and waste products are automatically broken down and disappear. The suit also balances the oxygen levels in the body. The helmet can teleport the wearer anywhere on the planet by entering the coordinates, in much the same way as we do now through Google Maps, except that you are physically moved there. It can also be set for space flight to another planet. The helmet dematerializes and rematerializes the body through nanotechnology, exactly as on *Star Trek*. The helmet also has the ability to enhance thought and interact with computers, so that it becomes possible to fly a spacecraft just by thinking. This is all accomplished by reverse-engineered nanotechnology.

VIRTUAL REALITY

The scientists can create virtual reality scenarios complete with voices and physicality for training purposes that are so realistic they are indistinguishable from real experiences. And the virtual experiences create new memory engrams so that they are remembered as real experiences.

The virtual reality technology is also used to set up group meetings with people on other planets. No more cell phones.

VIRTUAL AND REAL TORTURE

This technology is also used to inflict virtual torture on captives to elicit information. Although, according to Ileana, real torture also is frequently used by the Nazis to obtain information, just as with the Gestapo. Just as on Earth, the Nazi mentality is the same. She says that they do not hesitate to torture, maim, and kill, even children, whatever gets the job done. They commonly use blackmail that is based on their comprehensive personal computer records on everyone. Ileana claims that the Nazis create and sell sex slaves to other civilizations. These abuses are used just to get cooperation for missions. And when necessary, they will turn slaves into cyborgs just to be able to sell them off planet. So it seems that the interplanetary apple does not fall far from the earthly tree. Or perhaps, the fascist movement in the forties really originated elsewhere in the solar system. Certainly, the widespread pedophilia phenomenon being revealed lately on Earth does seem to have originated with a different species. Real human beings cannot torture and abuse children. It's just not in our DNA, which was created by the Elohim.

HYPERSPACE

In a later interview, Ileana said that the Dark Fleet has developed amazing technology that allows them to enter a "jumpgate" from their fighter aircraft! In other words, the pilot can press a button and enter a portal that takes the craft and its occupants to a distant planet. This is remarkable. It brings to mind the scenes in *Star Wars* where the pilot has that capability. This movie premiered in 1977, which would mean that George Lucas knew about jumpgates, perhaps in the early seventies. Lucas has been suspected of obtaining information from a secret source. See my book *Alien World Order*.

14

Supersoldiers

What a tragic realm this is, he reflected. Those down here are prisoners, and the ultimate tragedy is that they don't know it; they think they are free because they have never been free, and do not understand what it means.

PHILIP K. DICK

AGE REGRESSION

Perhaps the most amazing feat developed and performed by the ICC scientists is age regression. They can abduct individuals of any age, take them off planet, and force them to live for years under their control, employed by them to do specific jobs based on an agreed-to contract. The abductee would continue to age normally for those years. When the contracted time period had elapsed, they would "blank-slate" the person's memory so that it would all be forgotten and then regress the individual back to the precise moment that the contract was signed (see appendix A). At that point, the abductee would once again assume his or her original age at that moment of time. Anyone around him or her would not notice any change in age or demeanor. The person would just resume his or her life in the younger mind and body. It would be just as if that time spent off planet had never happened!

This is being done routinely by the German ICC scientists. But the memories persist, and in many cases, they resurface, and the missing-time stories are being told. The most common version of this is the Twenty-and-Back Program, which is mostly used with supersoldiers. These "enlistees" are frequently already in the military to start with and are given the opportunity to refuse the contract. This was the case with James Relfe, Kevan Trimmel, and others who are now coming forward. However, in other cases, the time served can be much longer. Bradley was taken for fifty-five years. And in some cases, as with Tony Rodriguez, it is forced labor and becomes a form of slavery. In any case, it is time wasted because even if the abductee is taught new skills, those skills can't really be applied after the person is returned because the memories are blank-slated. So a person might be left with unconscious new skills, but the experiences can't be put on a résumé.

TOTAL RECALL

Every once in a while, a movie is released that portrays an entire top-secret scenario masquerading as fiction. This was certainly the case with *Close Encounters of the Third Kind,* written and directed by Steven Spielberg. I made the case for that in my book *Secret Journey to Planet Serpo.* In the film, twelve military men were portrayed in orange jump uniforms waiting to board an alien craft to travel to the alien planet. The Serpo event was above top secret, but apparently the whole story had been given to Spielberg by someone in the Defense Intelligence Agency, and he wrote the entire screenplay in one weekend at the Sherry-Netherland hotel in Manhattan, which means he was working off a secret document of some type, since most screenplays require several months to develop.

Total Recall, starring Arnold Schwarzenegger and Sharon Stone and released in 1990, is a very similar case. It was based on a 1966 short story written by Philip K. Dick titled "We Can Remember It for You Wholesale." So many of Dick's novels and short stories have been prophetic and made into films that one would have to say that he appeared to have some sort of subconscious pipeline to actual secret and future events. (For instance, see the movies *Paycheck, Minority Report, Blade Runner, Radio Free Albemuth, Screamers,* and *A Scanner Darkly* as well as the television series *The Man in the High Castle.*) And his life was so short and unreal (married five times, three children, forty novels, and a great many short stories, dead at fifty-three) that this type of brilliant mental chaos would indicate that there is something else operating in his psyche, that is, that he was probably getting his ideas from some type of psychic or intuitive insights.

In 1966, who would have believed that selected memories can be easily wiped from the mind by corporate memory experts and that a slate of fictional but totally believable memories could be implanted to function as a pretend vacation trip? Certainly, everyone who went to see *Total Recall* in 1990 would not have believed it was possible. That audience, which included myself, viewed the movie as highly entertaining but a total fantasy. And further, who would have then believed that there was a sizable human city underground on Mars, built down there because the surface air was too thin to breathe, a city that was run as a profitable corporate enterprise, mining valuable minerals and shipping them all over the galaxy? Or that there was frequent human tourism to Mars? Or that the taxicabs in that Martian city were self-driving, although they seemed to be driven by human mannequins who could converse intelligently with the passengers? All of that, and much more, is happening on Mars now. We already have the self-driven cars here on Earth, although they haven't yet put the mannequins behind the wheel. That would make sense just to pacify other drivers, who might panic if they happen to pass a car without a driver.

JUMPED WITHOUT A PARACHUTE

In my first book, *The Secret History of Extraterrestrials,* I included a chapter titled "Man and Superman," about Andy Pero, born in 1969, who was one of the earliest supersoldiers. That chapter was written around 2005, although the book was published in 2010. Pero, a superb natural, multitalented athlete, was trained by his controllers to jump out of an airplane without a parachute! He lay on the ground unconscious for about an hour and then got up and walked away! He was then trained as an assassin by the Illuminati, but he finally rebelled and sought counseling after completing about ten missions. Since then, the supersoldier program has expanded, although nobody really knows how many of them are now walking around in our midst. But several others have now overcome their suppressed memories and recalled the details of their training and their missions, and they have stepped forward to publicly reveal this information.

Several of them were trained for conventional warfare roles and attached to military units on Earth and elsewhere in the solar system. It wouldn't be surprising to find them in numbers in such highly specialized units as Navy SEAL teams. But mostly, their talents seem to be prized for covert assignments, frequently for assassinations. Regardless of where they end up, in almost every case they are working for the Illuminati, one way or another, and that's why they are all subjected to MK-ULTRA mind control. Pero's life was threatened several times after he went public, but ultimately they found that they had succeeded all too well in creating a Frankenstein, as Pero estimated that he had to kill fifteen of his handlers before finally escaping from the program.

CREATED FOR THE JOB

Randy Cramer is a special case. Rather than having been identified as a likely candidate for the supersoldier program, Randy was created for it and was perhaps one of very few examples of prenatal recruitment, although by now they may be growing them in numbers.

Cramer was essentially created in a petrie dish. He says that he "was engineered in a laboratory from the ground up on Planet Earth." Like a new model Buick, he was "built in a better way." His outcome was very successful, whereas the soldiers created by the Monarch Solutions trauma-based mind-control system tend to be more fragile (see chapter 16, p. 170). The process of "genetic augmentation" while still in the womb has many advantages. He says he was made "faster, stronger, smarter." And anyone who knows him would definitely agree with that assessment.

Cramer was essentially born into the Marine Corps. Apparently, his parents knew that was his destiny from birth, and so he became a marine at seventeen. He was immediately combat-trained and deployed to the MDF as part of Project Moonshadow. Cramer was involved in several skirmishes on Mars. Typically, in battle he wore a light, protective undergarment gravity suit, over which he wore high-tech body armor powered by hydraulics. This was a sort of exoskeleton, probably somewhat similar to the one worn in the movie *Avatar*. In this suit, he could outrun the native wildlife, some of which were terrifying. He speaks of giant spiders, lizards, centipedes, and other large animals underground and smaller creatures that burrowed in the deserts. These were seen through the window of the spacecraft that landed on Mars in 1962. But, for the most part, he says that the flora and fauna are very similar to that on Earth. The sky is blue. Cramer says the normal gravity on Mars is only four-tenths that of Earth, but that it's normalized in the gravity suit. The air is basically breathable, similar to that of Earth at about 19,000 feet altitude. This would equate to the summit of Mt. Kilimanjaro. The surface temperature is very cold, but it's comfortable in the suit. In the base at Aries Prime, gravity plating is built into the floors, bringing the gravity to 1 g, just as on Earth. He says that the size of the base is about 150,000 square feet and that it is about 90 percent underground.

EXTENDED FAMILY

The native Reptoid population has been on Mars about one hundred thousand years. Cramer says they are "5.5 to 7.5 feet tall, fierce big lizard men, sandy colored (tan to brown)." They have an advanced understanding of science and tech, but they live in tribal communities. They are a blend of advanced tech knowledge with basic primitive living, like the Amish. They prefer the simple life because they experienced near self-destruction at one time. Cramer was captured, along with his squad, and they were kept prisoners for about six months. They lived as members of the community and were treated decently, like extended family. They lived on giant salamander tails mixed with fungi, moss, and grasses. He says it tasted like mud. The Reptoids actually speak decent English with a thick accent. They prefer that humans don't try to pronounce their language because how you speak is very important and if it is not pronounced correctly, it borders on being insulting. They are highly psionic and can use telepathy. They use their psi abilities in battle because they prefer hand-to-hand combat in which second-guessing your opponent gives you an advantage. Cramer says they have to have a reason to fight (e.g., "fight to right or fight for truth"). They preferred that his squad pick English names for them, which they then recognized. He said they did wear clothing consisting of finely milled fabrics, almost like silk. Cramer says the Reptoids and his men grew to respect each other during their captivity, and ultimately they became friends and signed a treaty.

INTERPLANETARY MEETINGS

Cramer says that there is a space station orbiting Jupiter that is used as a place for interplanetary and intergalactic negotiating. The main rooms on different floors are about a mile in circumference and can accommodate creatures of all sizes. He has seen humanoids there who are genetically related to us but are seventy feet tall! Cramer claims that he did interact with twenty- to thirty-foot-tall creatures, as well as dog-faced canine creatures who walk upright. They are doglike and they growl, but he had a translator box. He has seen feline species, cetaceans, plasma creatures, mineral rocklike creatures who are upright and bipedal, and even Bigfoot. He says he has been there about twenty-four times and has signed a lot of treaties. He says, "We have entered into many agreements that are socially and economically involved, as well as arrangements for intergalactic trade. Some of our chief exports are children's clothing for small people and robes. They like earth fashion; we make better stuff because we're better at manufacturing. There is also manufacturing on Mars."

MED TECH

The MDF military people eat cafeteria food at Aries Prime. They sometimes get strawberry pie with fake strawberries that taste real, but the coffee is imported from Earth and is excellent. The Aries Prime facility also uses some highly advanced medical technology. The regen tanks use holographic cellular regeneration that uses a person's genetic code to get damaged cells to conform. The field hospitals include "med beds" that can restore limbs, sometimes in hours. They can fix destroyed bodies and even cancer. Anything can be regenerated in these tanks. The entire body can be restored to a younger, healthier condition, theoretically forever. There are some officers on Mars who date back to World War II and are over one hundred years old. The colonists are told that there is no more planet Earth, so they are not seeking to return.

The technology is very closely guarded. Cramer is in the process of seeking patents here on Earth. He says, "We have to build it from the ground up. It's not cheap—startup costs would be over 24 million dollars." He is working on it and thinking ahead. You can find out more at Cramer's website, Earth Citizen Consulting.

15

The Slave Trade

This vision of a "peacetime Reich" was thus based on the existence of millions of permanent slaves, who were neither political opponents nor so-called "racial enemies." Because of economic necessity, they would be kept in camps all their lives—with "women in brothels." This empire of slaves, which was to stretch all the way to the Urals, would be the basic energy source of a Europe that had to prepare to conquer the greatest enemy: the United States of America.

ALBERT SPEER, *INFILTRATION*
(SPEAKING OF HITLER'S PLANS)

The slave trade in the solar system and beyond is rampant. Just as on Earth at Krupp and in Nordhausen, the Nazis depended on slavery to get the grueling work done. This dependence on slavery by the Nazis stems from their original astral modification by the Archons (see chapter 2). It is built into their DNA. It was seen in its most brutal manifestation in their treatment of the Hereros in German West Africa, as discussed in chapter 5, and of the Jews in Nazi Germany. The Nazis are literally a separate subspecies and are actually proto-human since they have no compassion for humans. Corey Goode, David Wilcock, and Emery Smith engaged in a comprehensive roundtable discussion of solar system slavery in a video called "Disrupting Draco Domination," an episode in the *Cosmic Disclosure* series. But there are now several other videos on YouTube on this subject. It really is an indefensible practice, since it wouldn't take much away from profit to provide the basic human needs for a working population. But the Nazis are indifferent to human suffering since they view humans as semi-animals who can be worked to death just to get a job done. Hitler has said this publicly. It is most revolting when it involves children and when it uses women as sex slaves, and it is in these practices that it becomes clear that the Nazi slave dealers are really proto-human.

In previous historical versions of human enslavement, such as in Imperial Rome and in the Old South in America, slaves were allowed to retain their dignity. It was mainly an economic matter, and in both cases slaves were frequently treated as a part of the family.

At its roots, enslavement is almost exclusively a male practice, and it derives from the patriarchal and misogynistic substrata of some human civilizations. But in its Nazi manifestation, it is beyond that since it is based on Archontic soul modification, which is totally indifferent to human pain and suffering.

A SLAVE ABDUCTION

Tony Rodriguez was abducted at nine years of age and was forced into a Twenty-and-Back Program. It was not voluntary, and he was not offered a contract, unless he signed it when he was in a drugged state and doesn't remember. He was abducted into a Nazi program as a slave because he had dared to embarrass one of his schoolmates, whose father happened to be high up in the Illuminati ranks. When the boy pointed Rodriguez out to his father in the school cafeteria, his fate was sealed. That night he was abducted by Grays, taken onboard a craft, and "processed." Unlike others in the program who were valued because they had military experience, Rodriguez was destined for enslavement right from the start. He woke up on a table at an air force base, which he later learned was near Seattle. He had to wait there until they had ana-lyzed his blood and determined the nature of his genetics. He was then drugged and mind-controlled in the MK-ULTRA program. Initially, he was "sold" to a connected individual in Seattle as a slave in that house-hold, where he was valued because of his psychic capabilities. Then after a few days, he was drugged and put on a plane and taken to Santa Marta, a Caribbean port in Colombia. There he was used as a sex slave in some sort of pedophile operation. He remained there for three years, until puberty.

SUICIDE BOMBER

Then, back in Seattle, Rodriguez was taken through a jumpgate to the LOC on the moon. As previously discussed, the LOC was constructed and controlled by the Nazis. He now recalls having been drugged again and put through a series of surgeries, mostly in an unconscious state. He was then put in front of a computer screen and trained to become a sui-cide bomber in the war between the Mars Marines and the Insectoids. His training curriculum at the LOC included going through a practice run in an arena where he was loaded with explosives and instructed to run toward and collide with a small Insectoid. Somehow, he survived that, but some others did not. They had to be reassembled in a regenera-tion tank.

Rodriguez was then shipped off to a forward base on Mars with about fifty others to join in actual combat against the Insectoids. They were all supplied with environmental suits, which included built-in tour-niquets, in the event of being wounded. He was sent on three missions. In the third one, his arm was bitten off by an Insectoid. Many of his friends were killed. He limped back and encountered a Mantid being, who questioned him. This creature was different from the Insectoids and seemed to be in charge. Evidently, the Mantids are more mentally and psychically powerful than the Insectoids. According to an online resource, "Mantids are man-sized praying mantises with humanoid proportions, triangular heads with large wraparound eyes, and long bent arms. They are rarely seen except in the company of Reptilians or Greys aboard ships. Their consciousness is unemotional, calculating, but extremely proficient in technical matters. They likely work as technicians specializing in consciousness manipulation, timeline alteration, and dimensional engineering."

The Mantid put him into a trance and accessed his subconscious memories. He could see his childhood home. Rodriguez begged for his life. The Mantid took pity on him and applied a tourniquet. This capacity was built into his suit, but he did not know how to use it. Then one of the small Insectoids bit off his foot. As sunset approached, Tony limped back toward his lines, hopping as best he could. Fortunately, he encountered a Space Marine, who said to him, "You are going to see a purple sunset!" The Marine carried him back, where he was put into a regeneration tank, in which he regrew his arm and foot. Rodriguez says that the small Insectoids were ugly creatures, unlike the Mantid. This testimony conforms with that of Cramer, who mentioned that the Mantids used the smaller Insectoids to do the fighting.

THE CERES MINING FACILITY

It was now 1989 and Rodriguez had turned seventeen. He was taken back to Aries Prime, where he was put through some more testing. He then joined in some more battles against the Insectoids in which he was issued a railway gun and a white uniform, which identified him as a slave. That assignment was canceled after a few days, and he was then put through a jumpgate to Ceres. Ceres is actually an asteroid in the asteroid belt, but has a spherical configuration, so it closely resembles a planet and is considered a dwarf planet. It is actually an oblate spheroid. Although Ceres is the largest object in the asteroid belt, it is only 587 miles across. A day on Ceres is about nine Earth hours. It has a revolution period around the sun of 4.6 years because it has a much wider orbit. Scientists believe that Ceres actually has more water than Earth.

Upon arrival on Ceres, Rodriguez was greeted by a couple of hundred Nazi soldiers, who evaluated the new arrivals and assigned them to jobs, much like the arrivals at Auschwitz. If anyone did not like his assignment, he was shot. Rodriguez says that there was a pyramid on Ceres and that underneath it were the ruins of an ancient colony that the Nazis had adapted to their own purposes as a mining operation and a residential community.

Rodriguez says that there were small towns all over Ceres, and they were all part of the Fourth Reich. He was assigned a cubicle-sized apartment. It was essentially a prison without bars. Some of the inhabitants had been born there and lived there all their lives. Initially, he had to work as a miner. The workers had to shout *sieg heil* and salute their officer every morning, and then were taken on a train to the work site. He says that there were swastikas in many places. Eventually, he was promoted to do repair work on an old garbage scow that docked there, and he became a welding specialist, operating high-tech automatic welding machines. When that ship was taken out of service, he started working on the newest model of the "Pumpkin Seed" craft that docked there at Ceres. He became good at his work. He was promoted and started to actually get paid.

ALWAYS COMPETITIVE

Rodriguez says that the officers in charge on all these projects always used a competitive system, pitting one worker against another and rewarding the best one. It was always the "carrot-and-stick" approach. Eventually, it became just like a regular job, and he got used to it. He worked on freighters that carried cargo all over the galaxy, and he visited many other planets. But if you tried to run away, you got shot. Rodriguez says that the population on Ceres was mainly civilians and families living in small towns all over the asteroid, in some cases, all their lives. The Nazi soldiers were like overlords.

He said that there were lots of females, many of them in their twenties, who primarily worked on the large freighters that docked there.

Many of them were citizens of Ceres. On one occasion, he got lost and had to ask for directions at a bar in a town, where he became friendly with a worker at the bar. He learned that it was part of a brothel, and eventually, when he learned how to get there, he became a customer. He became friendly with many of the women, most of whom were European. They told him that their customers were mostly ETs. He got friendly with one girl when they had to walk about two hundred yards to the train together and so had plenty of time to talk. Ultimately, she became his girlfriend.

Rodriguez says that the Nazi men were all bullies. They picked on everybody, including associates and girls. The slave workers all knew that they were on a Twenty-and-Back Program and were anxious to get home, although many of them had been told that the Earth had been destroyed. As the end of his sentence drew near, he had a lot more freedom. Ultimately, he was returned to the place from where he had been taken, and he became a nine-year-old again. For a long time, he had difficulty adjusting back to Earth life. But it became easier as he recovered more of his memories. He is now writing a book.

Rodriguez has now recovered memories of having been on planets in the Pleiades and Orion system, asteroids in the Kuiper Belt, and on Phobos, Titan, a distant swamp planet hundreds of light years from Ceres, Jupiter, Pluto, and several others. He mentions that the Germans were mainly interested in trading for high-tech products, but their customers on other planets wanted Earth weaponry. They were supplied with weapons to be traded by picking them up on Diego Garcia in the Pacific. This is a tiny island with a landmass about the size of a large aircraft carrier because most of it is under the water surrounding the island. Presumably, the weapons were dropped off there by armament manufacturers from all over the globe, who then received high-tech products from distant planets in exchange.

16

The Revenge of Penelope Valkyren

Every country that has nuclear weapons is part of the program. Earth is not being run for humanity but for elites, and they are planning on leaving. They think they will be spared because they are allied with the Dracos. Not likely.

PENNY BRADLEY

The abduction of Penny Bradley at the age of four and her brutal treatment at the hands of her Nazi handlers seems unprecedented and horrible. And yet, it was standard practice for the MDF, which is subordinate to the Mars German High Command. To have treated an innocent four year old the way they did testifies once again to the evil depths of the hard-hearted Nazi protohumans. For them, it was just "business as usual." She was kidnapped in 1959 and taken to the CIA headquarters in Langley, Virginia. It will be recalled that in 1959, the director of the CIA was Allen Dulles, a Nazi sympathizer, a friend of Nazi spymaster Reinhard Gehlen, and also a member of the Knights of Malta. As a lawyer in New York in 1933, Dulles and his brother, John Foster, had traveled to Cologne and helped to arrange the financing for Hitler to become the chancellor of Germany.

169

Fig. 16.1. Ex-space pilot Penny Bradley (passport photo)

There at Langley, she says that all her memories were "wiped" so that she really didn't remember anything about her family or home. She was given Room #7, and that became her name. They then proceeded to commence the trauma-based mind-control system that they had perfected. This was called Monarch programming. Monarch Solutions has been a large subcontractor to the Nazi hierarchy. (For more information about this subject, see the book *Trance Formation of America* by Cathy O'Brien with Mark Phillips.) She was immersed in a whirlpool tub and brought close to drowning by the inhalation of water into her lungs. If she had died, they would have revived her by putting her into a regeneration tank. This technique later became known as waterboarding and was widely practiced by the CIA on suspected spies. This kind of trauma in childhood forces the human mind to take refuge in a safe place by creating an alternate personality that has no memory of the event, thus defending against it. This is called a "split," and this new personality, partaking of the person's DNA, becomes like a separate person, known as an "alter." It can be seen as the birth of a new person in the same body.

A DRESS FOR CHRISTMAS

After the tub immersion phase of creating an alter, they began to shoot Bradley! She recalls being shot in the head, the heart, and the back. The CIA handlers relied on her panic before being shot to create the alter. Between sessions, she was left alone, day after day, in an all-white room illuminated with artificial light, with no one to talk to. To prepare her for electrodes on her scalp, they shaved her head. She was frequently forced to remain naked while others were in the room. Her handlers were brown-and-green Dracos. If she refused to cooperate, she was electrocuted and then regenerated. This happened to her five times. This trauma-based treatment usually resulted in the subject developing paranormal powers, such as telepathy and remote viewing, which were encouraged. She remembers only one individual who was kind to her during this entire ordeal, a nine-foot-tall Draco! She was allowed to wear a dress only once, for a Christmas festival. When she turned six, they inserted a computer chip behind her ear, so she was now attached to a quantum computer. At nine, her traumas finally ended, but by that time, she had created many alters. She believes it was over thirty because now, at the age of sixty-two, she has already reintegrated twenty-eight into her central, soul-based consciousness. This is necessary because each of her alters had taken a piece of her consciousness in order to survive and function. And now, she is getting them back with the help of hypnosis.

MONTAUK AND THE TIME TUNNEL

Bradley says that there were incinerators at the Langley facility. These were used to dispose of children who could not survive the trauma. Bradley had an inner strength that got her through it. It was her ability to mentally remain at a distance from whatever was happening to her and to view it impassively. Bradley calls it "going multidimensional." That was what her handlers were looking for to qualify her for responsible jobs on Mars. She was taken to Montauk, New York, several times and used in the time travel experiments. That facility was also under German/Nazi control (see appendix B). The children there were put through a time tunnel to a particular point in the 1880s in front of a general store. Each time she was sent there, she was supposed to steal an apple from the store and bring it back with her. The tunnel had loops along the way that could snare the traveler and divert that person to a different time. She was instructed not to wiggle and to just focus on the end point to avoid the snares. She became very adept at that technique. The handlers wanted to know what had changed each time she went through. They wanted people who could change things in a previous time that would persist into the present. Each trip took about three weeks from beginning to end.

MARS

In 1964, at the age of nine, Bradley was taken to New York City to a particular building with a particular elevator. It was probably very similar to the one to which Andrew Basiago was taken in El Segundo, California, under Project Pegasus when he was a boy (see the "jump-gates" listing in appendix A). It functioned exactly the same way. After the elevator door had closed, another one opened up on the other side. In Bradley's case, the elevator took on an oval shape. The second door opened after twenty minutes, and she and her handlers found themselves on Mars. This was a jumpgate. Bradley then attended school on Mars for ten years with other kids from the Martian colony, all of whom had no parents and all of whom had genetic modifications. She says that they were all considered freaks. They all had Reptilian DNA and psi abilities. She says that the school system reflected the overall Teutonic/German disposition of the Mars colony. The math used base 60 instead of our base 10. Using this system, irrational numbers become rational. She was taught about the "electric universe" and quantum mechanics. Unlike how our system works, the students were all rewarded for becoming bullies. It was a prized attitude (i.e., be aggressive to your contemporaries, submissive to authorities). This prepared the children for living in a Nazi society, where killing without conscience was demanded and worshipping the führer was required. While she was in school, there was a major attack by Raptors (see page 173) and many of the children were killed. They were then able to time travel to before the attack and to successfully repel it.

BRADLEY BECOMES A VALKYRIE

After graduating from school, Bradley became part of a group of eight who all lived together, and she discarded her numerical name and became known as Penelope, which was her real name on Earth anyway. She had attended the school for ten years and so was ready for an assignment at the age of nineteen. She became a second lieutenant pilot in the Dark Fleet and took on the full name of Penelope Valkyren, a name associated with mythical tribe of female warriors, the Valkyries. In thirteenth-century Norse mythology, the Valkyries rode through battlefields of slain warriors and selected half of them for entrance into Valhalla, the hall of heroes in the afterlife (see plate 19). They were immortalized in Richard Wagner's opera *The Ride of the Valkyries*.

It seems that Bradley became immersed in Germanic heroism in her new role in the Dark Fleet. She wore a dark-blue flight suit, courtesy of the U.S. Navy, a black leather jacket, boots, and a jaunty leather cap. She flew a fighter jet similar to the F-15, but with a plasma engine. She got a new chip behind her ear that allowed her to communicate with her ship. She had survived a very arduous process, and so they knew that she was the best of the best.

RAPTORS, MANTIDS, AND GIANT SPIDERS

The German colonists in the 1940s encountered armies of Raptors when they first settled on Mars. The Raptors were terrifying dinosaur-like creatures, apparently descended from ancestors in the Jurassic period on Earth, who were over six feet tall, had huge jaws, stood on their hind legs, and had six-inch claws for hands. They were militarily organized and had high-tech abilities. By the time Bradley was on Mars, the old wars weren't really over and skirmishes continued in the southern hemisphere. Those Raptors remaining in the southern hemisphere had no high-tech knowledge but were fierce warriors.

The Raptors ate humans and could cut a person in half in one bite.

Fig. 16.2. The Mars Raptors are descended from the Earth Raptors.

They inhabited old sites and were very territorial. There were also colonies of Mantids, who also were still at war with the Germans. Bradley's assignment was to destroy nests of Raptors wherever they were found. She was also occasionally required to give air support for Marine contingents in their battles with the Mantids and to capture a Mantid whenever possible. This required being on foot, and on one such mission, she was pounced on by a giant spider and bitten. The spiders on Mars could be fifteen feet across. She says the venom was like liquid fire, but it didn't last long. She remembered nothing after that and woke up in a regen tank. She then recalled being interrogated by Mantids and Dracos, and she says that she learned to just open up her mind and let them take whatever information they wanted.

Since Bradley was genetically modified, she was not allowed to have a lover. But others were having them, and she fell in love with another pilot. They had an affair until he was captured by the Raptors. She went on a mission and found that the Raptors were having him for dinner. The shock and panic she experienced caused her to press the wrong button, and the computer fired all her weapons at once by mistake, which killed everyone, including all the human captives. The computer then sent a message back to the MDF describing the incident. Her superiors felt that this episode meant that she was becoming emotionally unstable, and she was transferred out of the Dark Fleet into the Nacht-Waffen as punishment (see below). At that point, she had been on Mars for twenty-five years. The year was now 1990. In that year, the Raptors in the northern hemisphere were wiped out with a neutron bomb, which is a nuclear weapon that kills biological entities but leaves the physical superstructures intact. The Raptor colonies in the southern hemisphere were still alive and active, but had no high-tech capabilities.

NACHT-WAFFEN

In the Nacht-Waffen, Bradley became a navigator and was assigned to a large transport ship used to carry slaves and cyborgs to various planets in the solar system. Also, they carried prisoners of war back to the ICC, where they were turned into cyborgs instead of killing them. This was a profitable operation. Her job was not really to navigate but to watch for hazards in space that might affect the propulsion of the craft. Bradley says that space is not really empty. There are electromagnetic currents in space. And there are "critters" in space that feed off the electromagnetic energy of the craft, and they can clog the engine and reduce the power. Small critters are not a problem, but some are like the icebergs in the Atlantic, objects larger than the spacecraft that have to be avoided. The navigator has to watch out for these hazards and others and warn the pilot. There were three navigators on the ship she was assigned to, two women and one man. They had all been troublemakers and were there as a demotion. The genders had separate quarters. They worked ten-hour shifts. Bradley was given a new chip. The chips made the people a part of the ship, so that the officer in charge always knew where they were. So they had no freedom but always remained on the ship. It became their home because they functioned as part of the ship. Bradley remained in the Nacht-Waffen for another twenty-five years. She had now been a Nazi conscript for fifty-five years and had served on Mars for fifty years. It was time to go "home" and become a four-year-old Earth-human little girl again.

She was taken off the ship after her Nacht-Waffen stint was completed and told that her shift was up. They had originally told her that Earth had been destroyed by a cobalt bomb, so now they had to confess to the lie. One wonders how Bradley would have reacted if she had known the truth all along. She was taken back to the jumpgate terminal at Aries Prime and sent back to New York City through the elevator.

A HARD LIFE

Penny Bradley is now sixty-two. She remembers being back in her bed. That would have been fifty-nine years ago, or 1960. Her life back on Earth has not been easy. When she started kindergarten, she told the teacher that she had been kidnapped by Martians. Her father was a straitlaced preacher for the Church of Christ. Her parents beat her when they got the report from the teacher. Bradley went to school with children from the labor camps that housed Mexican workers given visas to follow the fields as farmworkers. As she advanced in school, she argued with teachers about math, which was different from what she had been taught on Mars. She fought a lot, which surprised a lot of her female schoolmates. She says she had to adjust to a non-Teutonic society like America, where women were submissive, whereas on Mars they were treated as equals. That was the case in America in the latter part of the twentieth century, but it has changed radically now, especially with the advent of the #MeToo movement. This is characteristic of non-Fascist German culture. Whereas Hitler and his fascist cronies and the kaiser were typically strongly patriarchal and misogynistic, viewing women primarily as housemaids and mothers. This type of male-dominated society usually breeds rampant homosexuality, as was the case in Germany during both World War eras. A journal article published by Illinois Wesleyan University in 2011 says, "Robert G. Waite notes that Nazi dogma, by 'denigrating females, encouraged the maturing adolescent to focus on the beauty of male personality and body.' Misogyny thus reinforced homoeroticism in the Wehrmacht."

So Bradley had emotional problems and depression. Every year, guys in dark suits would show up and administer IQ tests. She performed way ahead of her schoolmates, and in 1973, at the age of seventeen, she was awarded a full scholarship to Cornell University. Predictably, her father objected, and she had to go to a junior college, where she graduated with a 3.0 grade point average. Her first husband beat her and broke her neck in 1977. She has three children and two grandchildren. Her father died in 1980, and her mother remarried to a warrant officer in the army. Her mother made efforts to suppress Bradley's abilities and disowned her four times. They barely speak now. She found out that her mother has O negative blood, which explains a lot.

An article published on the internet, written by James Vandale in November 2011 says,

Rh-negative women and men have several 'Unusual Traits' that Rh-positives don't. Some call them Reptilian Traits. They are as follows:

- An extra vertebra (a "tail bone"). Some are born with a tail (called a "cauda")
- Lower than normal body temperature
- Lower than normal blood pressure
- Higher mental analytical abilities
- Higher negative-ion shielding (from positive "charged" virus / bacteria) around the body
- High sensitivity to EM and ELF fields
- Hyper vision and other senses

BRADLEY'S REVENGE

Bradley is now very much in demand as a speaker at UFO and super-soldier conferences, and she has created several videos that can be seen on YouTube. She is now revealing long-hidden secret information that has the potential to revolutionize our society. Her revelations can force dramatic changes in biology, science, and industry, especially transportation, in the space program, and in medicine, as we are beginning to comprehend what has been kept from us but is common on Mars. The secrecy keepers will now realize that they have created a monster who has the knowledge to bring down the structure that has so maltreated her. This will be the revenge of Penelope Valkyren.

17

The White Hats

The MDF works under the German High Command and side by side with several American Space Marines units connected with the Cabal. Traffic into Mars is very closely monitored. If a craft does not check in with the MDF, it is shot down. That's what happened to the early NASA Mars probes: they were shot down. This procedure is similar to tower operations at all American airports, except that planes are simply denied landing rights if they don't identify properly and are not shot down. All craft have to follow a flight plan to land on Mars and they need to check in with the MDF. The MDF monitors all ships once they are in Mars space. They have finally achieved territorial agreements that everyone agrees with. Presumably, these agreements were between the MDF and the U.S. Department of Defense. This probably became necessary because a joint United States–Soviet Union base was built on Mars in 1964, which eventually came under the jurisprudence of Solar Warden, the secret international space operation (see the "Solar Warden" section on page 184).

According to the former space pilot Penny Bradley, the Germans are trying to create a master race on Mars, and while that is in process, the planet is a police state. There is no freedom for anyone on Mars. Most of the citizens have chips in their brains, and their thoughts are monitored by a central quantum computer. If their thinking starts to wander to dangerous areas, they experience a sharp pain. The Germans want to create a race that is smarter than, and superior to, the human race on Earth. That effort is what was behind the so-called Brain Drain of the 1960s. The Germans, through the MILABs program, were abducting highly intelligent science and engineering professionals and taking them to Mars and Ceres, where the Germans could increase their IQs with certain electromagnetic enhancements and injections of drugs. The two colonies were in competition to create the smartest people. The Nazis always create competitive situations to push the winner's results even higher. In this case, the Mars colony ended up with the cream of the crop of an entire generation, while on Earth that same generation was deprived of those people and consequently was made "dumb and dumber."

Mars is now essentially a slave colony. The only humans allowed on Mars are slaves. Aries Prime has a quantum computer that is self-aware. Eventually, the quantum computer will run the society, and it will kill off all carbon-based life. Bradley says they encountered this syndrome on most of the planets they invaded. The quantum computers run the society, so individuals have to become cybernetic for personal survival. If they try to evade this control, eventually cyborgs will hunt them down and kill them. That's why Bradley is pessimistic about the future of the human race. Since the Dracos have embraced artificial intelligence, she doesn't see how the Federation, or any human-based alliance, can defeat them. She says, "Their empire may be in decline, but they are still more powerful than anything we have. And there was no rebel alliance. There is nothing that can stand up against the Draco."

THE SECRET SPACE PROGRAM

Bradley's pessimism about the future of the human race is understandable. If the Dracos succeed in integrating artificial intelligence into human society, then the cyborgs will take over and a silicon-based population will prevail over our carbon-based civilization. However, in my last book, *Alien World Order,* I made the case for a growing awareness about the tactics of the Reptilians and their puppets, the Illuminati, and the need for raising human consciousness so that we can repel artificial intelligence and transhumanism. If consciousness can be raised to a high enough degree, then we have a chance. The U.S. military is still dominated and controlled by the Cabal. But there is a growing population of "white hats" in the military ranks who are rebelling against Cabal control and are taking a stand for the human race. And we are now getting substantial assistance from our friends in the galaxy. Perhaps most importantly, we are now rapidly developing quantum computing at major universities and research facilities, which is filtering down to large advanced aerospace, medical, and hi-tech companies.

Bradley may not have been aware of what had been happening behind the scenes in the American military-industrial complex when she made that remark about the empire's decline. Apparently, she believed that the Cabal was still in charge and working with the Nazis in Antarctica and on Mars. On the surface that does seem to be the case. She knew about the Alliance* and the Federation and evidently was aware of Solar Warden. But she may not have had the latest information about how Solar Warden had grown in terms of both technology and membership.

WILLIAM TOMPKINS

Going back to the beginning, the U.S. Navy had German-speaking spies embedded with the Vril and Thule scientists in Munich who were working on antigravity craft in the late 1920s. Then, in the 1930s, when the Reptilians had made an agreement with Hitler, naval spying continued, giving the SS engineers timely data on new

---

*According to Corey Goode, "The Sphere-Being Alliance is fighting the current controlling elite known as the Cabal or Illuminati who exist on Earth at this very moment. They are human E.T. star systems. There are events and battles occurring above our atmosphere involving the Secret Space Programs and Break Away Civilizations. The people of Earth have been in debt slavery, mind controlled, sickened, and lied to in order to control the masses. We have had technologies suppressed from us that would change our lives. The Alliance is here to help humanity evolve out of this lower frequency." Apparently, the Alliance is sympathetic to the causes of the Federation, but is much smaller.

antigravity craft. The spies had originally been sent there by Admiral Rico Botta, who was from Australia, and so they had not been brainwashed at the U.S. Naval Academy. That was important because Secretary of the Navy James Forrestal had placed him in that position for that very reason. Forrestal apparently knew about how the academic curriculums in our military academies had been influenced and doctored by fascist academic infiltrators. For example, as Bradley had previously mentioned, the Nazi scientists on Mars were using base 60 math, which eliminated irrational numbers, while we were still using base 10.

All this information comes to us from William Tompkins in his recent book *Selected by Extraterrestrials*. In his book, Tompkins describes how he and his fellow aerospace engineers at Douglas Aircraft Company in Santa Monica, California, in the fifties were charged with using that spy information and meeting in a top-secret think tank at Douglas to design a U.S. Navy fleet of spaceships to counter what the Nazis were doing (see plate 20). What was perhaps most remarkable about those early days of the U.S. spaceship design sessions was the help the engineers were getting on the project from two attractive Nordic extraterrestrial women who knew much more than our engineers. Tompkins himself was receiving mental flashes of information and data, which he learned to rely on and which influenced the designs. This was the beginning of the American Secret Space Program.

Evidently, the Nazis on Mars were aware of the progress the American aerospace engineers were making in the 1950s and 1960s, and that was the real reason for the Brain Drain (see page 179). The American scientists were certainly not getting any help from NASA, where, starting in 1960, von Braun put the brakes on American engineering and slowed down progress drastically, while the German Paperclip scientists enjoyed their "vacation" in sunny Florida. It was only because of the push given to NASA by Kennedy in 1963 that we did succeed in putting men on the moon (see plate 21).

RENEGADE ENGINEERS

But the Brain Drain wasn't affecting this band of renegade engineers at Douglas. Tompkins didn't even have an engineering education. But he was perhaps the most effective member of the Douglas think tank because he seemed to be getting vital information from within, and it was being recognized and used by his associates. And he was helped by two beautiful extraterrestrial assistants in high heels. He was in the think tank for twelve and a half years, beginning in March 1951, working with such eminent engineers as W. B. Klemperer and Elmer Wheaton. He was transferred to engineering by the president of Douglas in April 1951, as a draftsman. He was asked to begin a study of aliens and government secrecy about our contacts with them. They also wanted him to design a naval moon base and other naval planetary bases. He was promoted to associate engineer after only six weeks in the tank. This allowed him to get married in September of that year. In December of that year, he established a requirement for naval space-ships and began designing and making the drawings for craft that were a kilometer in length. This was the inception of the Solar Warden craft (see plate 22). Tompkins worked for various aerospace companies after leaving Douglas in 1963, including North American Aviation, Rocketdyne, TRW, American Jet Corporation, Lockheed Martin, and General Dynamics, and he was involved in innovative projects wherever he went. His inner talents were recognized and used.

In 1967, two years before the moon landing, everything began to change in the California aerospace industry. At that point, there were about four hundred thousand people involved in planning the moon mission. Tompkins says in his book, "But some of us felt that strange things were happening in the Apollo Moon program and in advanced space research technological development. Not just the continual operational delays by both NASA and thousands of contractors, but the horrible problems confronting the nuclear propulsion even at Rocketdyne and Nucleonics. Almost all of space research was encountering

Fig. 17.1. Apollo 20 astronauts on the moon

insurmountable problems. Not openly, but throughout the space industry. A feeling of indifference was building, as contracts were continually delayed or canceled because of inconclusive answers. . . . Even before
the Apollo made it to the Moon and the program stopped, thousands
were laid off." It was a dramatic example of how the Reptilians and the
Illuminati were able to completely control business in a particular industry. After the moon landing, when the astronauts were warned not to
come back, all aerospace activity in the country came to a complete halt.

Tompkins decided to build his dream house at Lake Tahoe and go
into the real estate business. But his female friend Jessica from Douglas
wouldn't let him retire. She appeared to him one night while he was
outside looking up at the stars. She told him, "What are you thinking,
playing architect in the woods when the whole planet is still under the
****control of those grays and reptilians and they're pushing it back into
the dark ages?" She then pulled some strings and got him a dream job
at TRW.

SOLAR WARDEN

But the Secret Space Program was very much alive and masked by incredible security. It grew internationally until it finally blossomed in 1980.

The white hats were now in key and influential positions. In 1980, the Solar Warden space fleet consisted of four fleets of ships, nine Earth-orbiting space stations, which were cloaked, sixty-three space-based research stations, and forty-seven planetary research stations on six different planets. These ships are typically cigar-shaped and two hundred yards in length, with some several miles long and capable of carrying hundreds of crew members and passengers (see plate 23). The smaller craft may have been built on modified nuclear submarine beds, probably in New London, Connecticut (see plate 24). But one whistleblower says that the larger craft are built in an underground facility at the base of the Wasatch Mountain Range in Utah. He claims that there are thirty thousand personnel working at that facility. The craft are armed with exotic electromagnetic weaponry and are capable of speeds up to four times the speed of light. Another whistleblower says that the large Solar Warden craft can reach the center of the galaxy in forty-five minutes! The fleet ships, space stations, and research stations all use electromagnetic shielding, which not only deflects projectiles and energy-based weapons but also has the ability to phase or cloak whatever it is shielding. It is all *Star Trek* on steroids! The program operates under the U.S. Naval Network and Space Operations Command and is international in scope. The United Kingdom, Canada, Italy, Austria, and Russia have all made contributions to the operating costs through parts and systems. The location of the headquarters is unknown, but it is believed to be at a secret military facility like Area 51, possibly in Utah, employing about three hundred administrative personnel. It supposedly operates under the authority of the United States and the United Nations.

Solar Warden was almost compromised when a computer expert from Scotland accomplished what is being called "the biggest military computer hack of all time." Gary McKinnon, then living in London, hacked into ninety-seven U.S. military and NASA computers over a thirteen-month period from February 2001 to March 2002. One of his hacks was into the Johnson Space Center, where he viewed a list of "non-terrestrial officers" being moved to the ships. Two of the ship names were the USSS

LeMay and the USSS Hillenkoetter. "USSS" stands for U.S. Space Ship. General Curtis LeMay was the chief of staff for the U.S. Air Force, and Admiral Roscoe H. Hillenkoetter was the first director of the CIA. Both of these men had connections to UFO investigation. McKinnon said, "I found a list of fleet to fleet transfers and a list of ship names. I looked them up. They weren't U.S. Navy ships. What I saw made me believe they have some kind of spaceship, off-planet." He also brought up a screen shot of a huge cigar-shaped craft hanging in what seemed to be space, with the Earth below. McKinnon had stumbled his way into Solar Warden files. He was indicted by a Virginia grand jury, but his extradition to the United States has been blocked.

According to "a reliable source" in the Open Minds website's forum, "All space programs are a cover that exists to deceive the people of this world. We have a space fleet, which is codenamed 'Solar Warden.' There were, as of 2005, eight ships, an equivalent to aircraft carriers, and forty-three 'Protectors,' which are space planes. One was lost recently to an accident in Mars orbit while it was attempting to re-supply the multinational colony within Mars. This base was established in 1964 by American and Soviet teamwork." The claim of a secret base on Mars was confirmed by a physicist named Henry Deacon, who had worked at Lawrence Livermore National Laboratory; he spoke to Kerry Cassidy and Bill Ryan of Project Camelot in 2007. Deacon said, "Transport is by two means: stargates for personnel and small items, spacecraft for larger items of freight. The alternative fleet is codenamed SOLAR WARDEN."

COREY GOODE

Corey Goode is doing more than anyone else to reveal accurate information about the Secret Space Program and the U.S. role. Because he was a supersoldier in the Twenty-and-Back Program who has now recaptured his memories, he has the standing to give us this information. Goode was considered an "intuitive empath" by his MILAB handlers and consequently was assigned to a research vessel, where he was able to attend interstellar meetings to use his talents to pick up unspoken intentions and strategies. He worked directly in the Solar Warden program. He says that the Solar Warden fleet was divided into a research and development sub-fleet and a military branch and that the personnel on the military craft were mostly American, but these ships also had some British, Canadian, and Australian crew members. The research-and-development craft were more international and included some German and Chinese scientists as well as crew and scientists of other nationalities. Goode was assigned to a research vessel. It was classified as ASSR, for Auxiliary Specialized Space Research. It was considered to be an ICRV ship, for Interstellar Class Research Vessel. It was named the Arnold Sommerfeld. This name would suggest that it was assigned by a German organization since Sommerfeld was a noted German theoretical physicist who had achieved great honors in his career and was widely regarded to be in the same category as Albert Einstein. Four of his doctoral students went on to win Nobel Prizes. These included Werner Heisenberg and Hans Bethe, both of whom became important in nuclear physics and worked on atomic energy projects in the forties. Sommerfeld rejected any Nazi affiliation, and consequently, like Einstein, is really admired internationally as a great figure in quantum physics. So it is really not so surprising that he would be chosen to have an antigravity ship named after him since his work in quantum physics played a major role in articulating the science that made the ship possible.

Goode was on the Sommerfeld for six years, during which time he dealt with many "off-world beings" and was rotated to Federation conferences that Soviet Space Program leaders were honored to be a part of. Goode says that Solar Warden was a "heavily naval program" in the beginning and even though the rank and file were recruited through the MILAB system, the officers were primarily U.S. Navy and very much believers in honoring their Constitutional oaths. The aforementioned whistleblower says that there is a top-secret Solar Warden educational and training facility near Medford, Oregon. This naval connection explains why the *Star Trek* crew conformed to naval traditions and practices and why the *Enterprise* was really considered a naval vessel, suggesting that Gene Rodenberry (creator of the original *Star Trek* series) had that information. It also explains why the engineers at Douglas Aircraft Company, including William Tompkins, had a naval connection. Tompkins reported to Admiral Rico Botta in the beginning, and the Douglas spies in Germany were also navy assets.

Much more can be said about the life and work of Goode, particularly his interviews and conversations with David Wilcock and Emery Smith, which are available as YouTube videos in the *Cosmic Disclosure* series.

THE LEGACY OF SPOCK

The existence of Solar Warden, an American spaceship fleet, holds out great promise that it can become the foundation of a force that will dispossess the Nazi authority in our solar system and ultimately stop the creation of cyborgs and the enslavement of humans. We now have the technology to roam the galaxy and, as Ben Rich* said, to "take ET home." We may yet be able to prove Penny Bradley wrong. We may be able to save carbon-based life and to prevent the takeover by artificial intelligence. We may be able to help create an interstellar human society in which we can all "live long and prosper."

Fig. 17.2. Leonard Nimoy as the character Spock from the television series Star Trek

---

*Ben Rich was the president of the Lockheed Martin Skunk Works. The Skunk Works helped develop our spaceships, and the Solar Warden technology. This remark was made in his farewell retirement speech in 1989.

A Review of German/Nazi Off-World Technology

The Nazi Technological Advantage

The remarkable off-world technology that the Nazis possess can be mainly attributed to their partnership with the Reptilian race known at the Reptoids. The Reptilians are the beneficiaries of thousands of years of scientific and technological discovery and innovation on their home worlds in Draco and Orion. I covered this in detail in my previous book, *Alien World Order*. Also, since they dominate and enslave alien races wherever their conquests take them, they have a built-in slave population, which they use for experimentation and development of their incredibly advanced technologies, as Josef Mengele did at Auschwitz. When they came to Earth, they applied their ancient practice of using a segment of the native population to turn against the larger planetary population to carry out their domination of the planet. This is how they manage their huge empire in this galaxy. That is how they sank Atlantis, and that is how they are managing the human population of Earth. As discussed in chapter 2, they selected the Germanic race to be their modern agents in this solar system, upon whom they showered riches and amazing science and technology in return for which they expected them to do their work for them, enforced by mind control. The following is an alphabetical overview of that technology.

Age Regression: The Nazi scientists routinely use this technique to return supersoldiers and slaves who have been abducted from Earth back to the precise age and time at which they were first taken. This is part of their time travel technology, which apparently keeps holographic records of moments of time, which is evidently how the Akashic Records are maintained. So the precise physical body at the moment of abduction can apparently be restored by dialing it into an age-regression pod. Ileana, the Star Traveler, says that it takes about two weeks in the pod, during which time the subject remains in an unconscious stasis. This is remarkable technology, and the implications are fantastic. It means that anyone can be regressed from old age to youth just by going into the pod. So it seems that the Fountain of Youth already exists! Ileana says that this process is aided by remarkable drugs.

Antigravity Craft: All the craft used by the Nazis for traffic to and from Base 211, the moon, Mars, and other points in the solar system and beyond use electromagnetic antigravity technology. It is used to propel gigantic freighters all over the galaxy. We also have antigravity craft used in the Solar Warden fleet, and it is believed to be employed on other U.S. aircraft, such as the B-2 Spirit stealth bomber and the TAW 50 fighter. Evidently the suppression of this information is controlled by the Cabal through the military-industrial complex.

Artificial Intelligence: The combination of quantum computing and nanotechnology makes true artificial intelligence possible. The Nazi-produced cyborgs at the Cybernetics Laboratory on Mars are now very advanced. They have eventually become self-aware and can now make independent decisions, and thus can operate starships and can populate and run colonies on other star systems. Once again, we were first made aware of these possibilities through a fictional device. In the movie

Blade Runner, released in 1982, starring Harrison Ford, and based on a story by Philip K. Dick, the blade runner's job is to track down cyborgs, called Replicants, who are "more human than human" and who can only be revealed to be cyborgs by a very sophisticated eye examination using very advanced equipment. Prophetically, the movie is set in 2019.

Cloning: The German scientists on Mars routinely use human cloning to create new bodies when necessary. It is a speeded-up system that duplicates a human body in a matter of days. Randy Cramer, a.k.a. "Captain Kaye," reports that his body was cloned and his consciousness and memories were inserted into the new body and that is how he was returned to a healthy, new, young condition when his twenty-year tour of duty in the MDF was completed. Presumably, his old body was discarded.

Free Energy: It is used by the Nazis on all their solar system bases and is based on scalar electromagnetics as first developed by the Serbian-American engineer and physicist Nikola Tesla. It is a way of extracting energy directly from the ether and converting it to electricity. This technology was first conceived by Tesla and used by the American inventor Thomas Bearden in his free-energy machine. It is based on corrections to James Clerk Maxwell's equations on electomagnetism. This is apparently the means by which all the suns in the universe derive their power. Tesla also developed the capability of sending free electrical energy through the air from a tower to users everywhere on the planet. This could only have been achieved by converting energy from the ether. Thanks to the American financier J. P. Morgan, who was backing Tesla, the tower was eventually destroyed because there was no way to make it profitable.

Holographic Disguise: ETs working with the Nazis have the ability to pull down a holographic disguise to make them appear human. It's not clear whether or not the human hybrids have this ability. But the Reptilians do use this technique. They generally don't like to use it because it takes too much energy.

Jumpgates: This technology allows the immediate movement of individuals, heavy equipment, and materials to a point anywhere in the solar system designated by GPS coordinates, just as in the movie *Stargate*. Jumpgates also permit movements forward or backward in time. Time travel jumpgates were used by the Nazis as early as the fifties at Montauk. The Cabal also has this technology, and it is controlled by the CIA. It was employed in Project Pegasus in the sixties in which Andrew Basiago and other young adults were sent to Mars from El Segundo, California, by a CIA intermediary (see appendix B). Basiago was also sent back in time to witness the Gettysburg Address by Abraham Lincoln. The UFO researcher Robert Dean reported that he witnessed a U.S. general being jumped from the United States to Australia by walking through a door. It can also be used to send people to underground locations.

Memory Storage and Cyborgs: Quantum computers are being used in the Cybernetics Laboratory on Mars and throughout the Nazi off-planet colonies. This technology makes true artificial intelligence possible since the computers can interact with tiny chips inserted under the skin behind the ear. It allowed Penny Bradley to actually become part of the onboard computer system on the freighter ship she worked on in the Nacht-Waffen. And this is how the cyborgs can display seeming intelligence, although they are really semi-robotic. Cyborgs called "alters" are frequently produced from individuals who have had their personalities split by trauma. This is why cyborgs do not have complete memories. The memories are stored on computers as small as chips. Thus these memory packages can also be used to animate clones or other cyborgs.

Mental Enhancement: The ability of the smart-suit helmet to enhance thinking is amazing. It is not clear how this works, but apparently the helmet emits high energy to the brain. This enhancement permits direct two-way interaction between the brain and quantum computers onboard the craft. Once this connection is established, the brain can now control the computer that flies a craft so that the craft can now be controlled just by thought! We have seen this technology before in the alien survivor of the Roswell UFO crash. It was noticed that somehow his suit controlled the craft. We have learned from Penny Bradley that she was able to pilot her Dark Fleet craft that way.

Nanotechnology: In the prophetic science fiction movie *Fantastic Voyage,* starring Raquel Welch and released in 1966, a submarine and medical crew are shrunk to microscopic size and inserted into the bloodstream of a dying scientist to save his life. This movie won two Academy Awards.

But such a voyage is not so fantastic anymore. An article published on the BBC News website on November 23, 2000, is titled "Nanocopters Leave the Drawing Board." The article says,

> The first microscopic "helicopters," which could one day carry out medical tasks inside the body, have been built and test-driven by scientists. The devices, no bigger than a virus particle, could eventually move around the human body, ministering to its needs or dispensing drugs. The metal rotors of the tiny machines are powered by the body's natural fuel, a chemical called ATP. When the biomotors were tested in the laboratory, they were able to drive the helicopters' propellers for up to two-and-a-half hours. This is an important first step towards producing miniature machines capable of functioning inside a living cell. The tiny helicopters consist of three parts: metal propellers and a biological component attached to a metal post.
>
> When the three components are mixed together, the tiny machines self-assemble. The biological material converts the body's biochemical fuel, ATP, into energy. This is used to turn the propellers at a rate of eight rotations per second. A team at Cornell University carried out the work. Carlo Montemagno who led the team said: "With this demonstration, we believe we are defining a

whole new technology. We have shown that hybrid nanodevices can be assembled, maintained and repaired using the physiology of life." This is only a first step as the technology is still very inefficient. Only five of the first 400 biomotors worked.

Eventually, the Cornell nano-biotechnologists sought to engineer biomolecular motors to run on light energy, with photons instead of ATP. They also planned to add computational and sensing capabilities to the nanodevices, which ideally should be able to self-assemble inside human cells. To underscore the importance of this research, it should be noted that it was financed jointly by the National Science Foundation, the Defense Advanced Research Projects Agency (DARPA), the Department of Energy, the Office of Naval Research, NASA, and the W. M. Keck Foundation, which has since founded a Department of Nanotechnology at Cornell.

That article appeared nineteen years ago. Since that first pioneering effort, nanotechnology has come a long, long way. The potential applications for life on Earth are revolutionary and endless, and nothing short of incredible. A scientist at the Cornell lab says, "The foreseeable future does include nanomachines that are very like today's computer chips, but with moving parts. This technology will allow people to build things like accelerometers for car air bags that are more reliable, cheaper, and less expensive than other designs; prosthetics for those who are deaf due to injury or disease to the cochlea; hand-held inertial navigation systems cheap enough to take on a camping trip; TVs that fill an entire wall, but are less than an inch thick, and with each pixel implemented as a triad of flappers moving 60 times a second; optical-fiber switching systems where the fiber itself is moved from one place to another." The metal found on the Roswell alien craft that could be wrinkled beyond recognition with hammers and even shot with a gun and that always returned to its smooth original condition was created by the aliens using nanotechnology.

The Nazis on Mars have been using nanotechology since the sixties.

Neurolinks: These are electromagnetic brain implants that link to quantum computers at ICC bases and onboard Dark Fleet ships. This allows the victim to be tracked unconsciously and all brain activity and communications to be recorded. They are etheric implants and can be removed by the right energetic techniques, but they can cause brain damage.

Quantum Computing: It was really nanotechnology that made quantum computing possible. Quantum computing deals with tiny subatomic particles that we had previously not been able to measure. But they are now measurable because of the development of new microscopes. Once they became observable, then it was noticed that how they were measured could change the value of the particle so that the measurement technique had to be factored in to determine the particle's real value. As computers became superfast, they could now deal with the actual values in this tiny world and could become much more accurate, so that the new computers can now deal with quantas of information instead of bits and bytes. A quanta incorporates all the characteristics of a particle, including its motion. These quanta are now called qubits and can be teleported.

Here on Earth, the use of nanotechnology is not yet in the realm of the miraculous. But it is on Mars. Thanks to the [German] Nazi's Reptilian friends, science and technology on Mars are eons ahead of what humanity has developed on Earth. As the Reptilians helped the Nazis in Antarctica to develop an amazing space program, so they now help them with science and technology on Mars. The German Nazi scientists are currently using nanotechnology to mass-produce cyborgs and all sorts of self-replicating products that can extend life, replace lost organs and limbs and permit human teleportation with or without spaceships. But according to Ileana, the Star Traveler, it is in quantum computing at the ICC Cybernetics Laboratory on Mars where nanotechnology is most miraculous. Ileana was taken to Mars as a teenager, and because of her remarkable language skills she worked in the Cybernetics Laboratory for twenty years. It is the nanotechnology at the lab that facilitates the computational speeds of several quadrillion floating-point operations per second. A quadrillion floating-point computations is called one petaflop.

There is evidence that quantum-computing technology is also already being used here on Earth by the secret military-industrial complex, also known as the Cabal. The computer system at the Oak Ridge National Laboratory in Tennessee, the Titan, is the fastest computer in the world. It has now reached twenty petaflops, which equates to twenty quadrillion floating-point operations per second! That makes this technology far beyond instantaneous, if that is possible, so that it is essentially undifferentiated from being "magical." There is no way that speed could ever have been attained by normal solid-state semiconductor technology, and so the Titan is probably a quantum computer using nanotechnology. It makes sense that the Nazi scientists on Mars would have begun secretly using their advanced technology on Earth, since the Fourth Reich essentially controls the Cabal.

Quantum Mechanics: This operation apparently uses scalar electromagnetics to propel spacecraft through the space-time plenum in which distance is erased, so that they can travel at up to four times the speed of light. The Nazis have been trading with distant planets all over the galaxy, including Jupiter, Pluto, the moons of Saturn, Ceres, and asteroids in the Kuiper Belt. Apparently, this technology is possessed by most civilizations in the galaxy, since Randy Cramer met with representatives from distant star systems at meetings on a Jupiter space station. Evidently, this technology is used in the helmets worn with the smart suits, since the wearer can transport himself or herself instantly to another location in the solar system and beyond. This is done through dematerialization and rematerialziation, exactly as on *Star Trek*.

Quantum Teleportation: The quantum entanglement of two subatomic qubits has permitted the teleportation of one of the particles to join the other when they are separated at distances of up to eight hundred miles.

That distance limit has now been far surpassed and basically erased. This teleportation is at the speed of light, but applies only to information and not to physical matter. The German scientists on Mars are somehow able to use this technique to connect the craft of the Dark Fleet with their headquarters without the use of radio, and it is instantaneous. As a pilot, Penny Bradley was able to actually become part of the onboard quantum craft computer and therefore to communicate with other craft and the headquarters with the simple implantation of a tiny chip behind her ear. That way, all communications within the Dark Fleet are immediate and automatic, can include captured visuals, and are automatically recorded no matter where in the solar system the ships are located.

Regeneration: The Nazis use this to restore damaged bodily parts and systems back to their original condition by immersion in the so-called regeneration tanks. This is how the soldiers and pilots in the MDF are kept perfectly healthy. This procedure uses nanotechnology and holographic cellular regeneration based on the DNA. In the case of the restoration of organs, arms, and legs, the system apparently rebuilds the physical cells on the astral models of the missing or damaged organs or limbs to conform to the DNA. Some people have claimed that the regeneration tanks use something called black or gray goo. Similar goo is seen as a by-product in laboratory experiments in nanotechnology on Earth. The regeneration tanks also can reportedly, at least in some cases, restore the dead back to life!

Replication: The ICC scientists on Mars have developed machines that can replicate anything. They are used to create complete meals or to make copies of complicated pieces of equipment, much like 3-D printers.

Smart Suits: This is amazing technology that was developed by the Nazi scientists at the Cybernetics Laboratory on Mars, which is really an ICC facility. These suits are lightweight and formfitting, and they are technological marvels. According to Ileana, the Star Traveler, the suits are totally protective against most weapons, whether physical guns or laser-energy or directed-energy weapons. The suits are created using nanotechnology and can protect against most kinds of directed or even generalized attacks. They automatically monitor all biological functions and are programmed to supply nutritional supplementation to the body when needed, without the wearer's conscious awareness. The suits also dispose of all biological waste by means of chemical dissolution and transformation. This also happens under the level of conscious awareness so that soldiers in these suits can focus on military operations without distraction. The suits are attached to quantum-computerized helmets that can transport the wearer to other planets in the solar system without the use of a spaceship!

Stargates and the Cosmic Web: According to Corey Goode, all the stars and planets in the physical universe are linked by electromagnetic energetic filaments. Goode refers to this network of filaments as the Cosmic Web. These links are sometimes referred to as wormholes. Because of these connections, it becomes possible to travel instantaneously from one star or planet to another through the Cosmic Web. In order to do that, it is necessary to determine precisely where on the planet or in the solar system the web filaments pass or terminate. These filaments are constantly shifting because of the movements, both by revolution and rotation, of the stars and planets, and so they coincide with different points at different times depending on where the movement path intersects with these bodies or points. According to Goode, these points can be precisely plotted using hyperdimensional mathematical formulas. They reveal the entrance and exit points on the Cosmic Web, which we know as stargates. Evidently, the Nazi off-world scientists have learned how to use these formulas to travel throughout the galaxy. It may have been made possible by their elimination of irrational numbers, which are used in base 10 arithmetic, and the substitution of base 60 mathematics, wherein all numbers become rational. We now know they use this system thanks to Penny Bradley. Consequently, with the help of quantum computing, expeditious travel among the stars has become easy for them, and what were formerly impossible distances to traverse have been reduced to short trips that depend only on stellar navigational requirements. They do have this connection from the moon and Mars to Earth, and this explains their frequent trips back and forth.

Transference of Consciousness: The ICC scientists have the ability to transfer the soul, which is really what creates consciousness, from one body to another. They can also keep it in an electromagnetic stasis chamber temporarily before inserting it into another body, which can be biologically created or cloned. I discussed this technology in my last book, *Alien World Order,* in which I reported that according to Robert Morning Sky, the Reptilian scientists under the queens of Orion developed this capability thousands of years ago and used it extensively. So it seems very likely that the ICC scientists obtained it from their Reptilian friends.

Walking through Walls and Invisibility: This capability, which has been reported in extraterrestrial abduction scenarios since the fifties, evidently is somehow related to increasing the vibratory rate of the physical body by some artificial device or enhanced mental power. Now, it seems that the off-planet Germans have this capability and that they are using it in MILABs. Invisibility has been achieved by a cloaking technique, probably using diffusive light-scattering cancellation. This is already working in laboratories here on Earth and is evidently more advanced in the German colonies.

APPENDIX B

Time Travel

From the testimonies of the ex-supersoldiers who have recovered the memories of their time on Mars and other planets and moons in the solar system, we have garnered a wealth of information about Nazi technology. These reports confirm what was already secretly known about Nazi scientific breakthroughs in Europe and the United States in recent times. They have developed the ability to travel in time. This is the result of their technological partnership with the Reptilians. There was absolutely nothing in Germany before World War I that demonstrated this capability. Up until the unification of Germany in 1871, they were preoccupied with political and economic matters. It was a gift on a silver platter by the Reptilians between the two World Wars, and so it was brought with the Germans to their ICC Cybernetic Laboratory on Mars in the 1960s and 1970s.

We first learned of it through information reported by coauthors Preston Nichols and Peter Moon in their book *The Montauk Project: Experiments in Time,* about what occurred in the underground base at Montauk on Long Island. The book was published in 1992, but it discussed events that began in the forties. The research into time travel began with the Philadelphia Experiment in 1943, where it was learned that invisibility of a naval vessel could be achieved by mental influence on a super-enhanced electromagnetic field around the vessel. Reportedly, the ship also reappeared forty years later off Montauk Point, suggesting that it briefly went through a time warp. The technical director of that experiment was John von Neumann, a brilliant German mathematician and scientist who had become an American citizen when he was invited to join the faculty of Princeton University in 1933 and so became a colleague of Albert Einstein, who was at Princeton at the same time. Von Neumann is credited with the invention of the modern computer. After World War II, he linked up with his German scientific contemporaries who were brought here under Operation Paperclip. That gave him access to "the enormous resources of the military-industrial complex which included the vast data base of Nazi psychological research that the Allies had acquired after World War II." This Nazi database included the contributions of the Reptilians that began in 1933 under Hitler. Von Neumann was fascinated with the computer-human interface and worked to link the human mind directly with computers. After the war, he was asked to begin a massive human factor study at the Brookhaven National Laboratory on Long Island, which became known as the Phoenix Project.

Von Neumann tried to link human thinking with radio equipment. Eventually, he was able to receive and store thoughts on crystal radio receivers as information bits. The thoughts could then be displayed on a computer screen and printed. These techniques were enhanced until a mind-reading computer was developed. This was the beginning of Nazi mind control. Congress then closed down the Phoenix Project after concerns were voiced about this sinister technology. But a well-funded secret military program resumed the work at Fort Hero, a closed air force base at Montauk, Long Island, where a huge SAGE (Semi-Automatic Ground Environment) radar antenna was still operative. In the experiments there, the researchers found that thoughts could be amplified electronically and could open up time portals, as was done in 1943. On August 12, 1983, a fully functioning time portal was opened up under human control at Montauk. But DARPA and the CIA already had that technology. They had been using it in Project Pegasus since 1968 (see below). By this time, the Martian German scientists were also using the technology routinely, and it then became secretly used at Montauk. And so in the sixties, it was folded into the CIA projects in time-space modification. The Montauk Nazi scientists then began using the portal to send street children into the past, some of whom never returned. Penny Bradley was sent to Mars through a Montauk portal. By this time, Allen Dulles, a known Nazi sympathizer, had become director of the CIA in 1953, and the entire U.S. program came under CIA control and direction. The Martian program was controlled by the German-dominated MDF.

According to Al Bielek, who was involved in the Phoenix Project, "The technology for the tunnels was given to us by cooperative effort of alien groups, primarily the Orion group, which involved reptilians, a sub group called the Leverons. A technical group, which provided most of the assistance, was the group from Sirius A. Very materialistic, scientific people. Perhaps not a bad heart but misdirected, because they had very long-term contracts with the Orions to provide them with the technical knowledge and assistance they needed. And they were working with our government in secret to work out mind-control techniques and technology and pushing for a highly automated, technical society which would be much easier to control than it would be the way it is now. But we're approaching that rapidly."

PROJECT PEGASUS

But the Montauk project was very late to the game. That is probably because, initially, they were not controlled by the CIA and apparently were not aware of the highly compartmentalized Nazi colony and technology on Mars. Whereas, according to Andrew D. Basiago's Project Pegasus website, "[This website is part of] a quest begun in 1968 by Andrew D. Basiago when he was serving as a child participant in the US time-space exploration program, Project Pegasus. Project Pegasus was the classified, defense-related research and development program under DARPA in which the US defense-technical community achieved time travel on behalf of the U.S. government—the *real* Philadelphia Experiment. Project Pegasus was launched by the U.S. government to perform 'remote sensing in time' so that reliable information about past and future events could be provided to the US President, intelligence community, and military."

As a young boy, Basiago was probably the first human who was teleported back in time, and he was actually photographed at his destination (see figure A.1)! In my article published in *Atlantis Rising* magazine in 2015, with the title, "Jumping through Space-Time," I say:

> The black & white photograph shows a boy standing alone in a clearing on the Gettysburg battlefield. He is wearing a men's Union Army parka, and shoes about four sizes too large.* He appears somewhat out of place since he is all alone. In the background, a large audience is assembled, and a dais is set up, while in the foreground a group of three men is in serious discussion. The photo purports to be the scene just before Lincoln began to deliver the Gettysburg Address on November, 19, 1863. The old photograph was discovered in a magazine by Andrew Basiago in 2003.

The photograph was an amazing confirmation of this historic event. The eleven-year-old Basiago had gone through a teleportation device in 1972 from a jerry-rigged basketball court at a high school in Cerillos, New Mexico.

Basiago says, "It was expected that the 140 American schoolchildren secretly enrolled in Project Pegasus would continue to be involved in

---

*Basiago's travel through the Time Tunnel was rough. He was bounced back and forth and eventually lost his shoes and one sock. So when he arrived in 1863 Gettysburg, he walked barefoot into the town and stood and peered through the window of a clothing store. A passing gentleman, seeing him barefoot in the cold weather, asked if he could help him. The store had many of the uniforms and clothes of the Union soldiers who had died in the horrific Battle of Gettysburg. The man took him into the back of the store and allowed him to pick out a men's Union jacket and socks and shoes, recovered from the battlefield.

Fig. A.1. Andrew Basiago (young boy alone, center) after being teleported back in time to 1863, photographed at Gettysburg on the day of President Abraham Lincoln's famous address.

time travel when they grew up and went on to serve as America's first generation of 'chrononauts.' The children found, however, that in the process of serving as child time travelers attached to Project Pegasus, they became America's time-space pioneers."

Unfortunately, that visionary goal was never realized because the Cabal, the secret military-industrial complex in America, which President Eisenhower had warned us about, remains opposed to disclosure and continues to serve the purposes and dictates of the Fourth Reich.

Basiago, now a fifty-eight-year-old attorney living in Seattle, Washington, has mounted a presidential bid for 2020. If he succeeds in becoming the president, he could usher in a fantastic new era in American technology and history. Basiago says, "Imagine a world in which one could jump through Grand Central Teleport in New York City, travel through a tunnel in time-space, and emerge several seconds later at Union Teleport in Los Angeles. Such a world has been possible since 1967–68, when teleportation was first achieved by DARPA's Project Pegasus, only to be suppressed ever since as a secret weapon. When my quest, Project Pegasus, succeeds, such a world will emerge, and human beings linked by teleportation around the globe will proclaim that the Time-Space Age has begun!"

Further Reading
and Viewing

Juango5. "UFOs in Washington, D.C.: July 12, 1952." Video on YouTube.

Miranda Lee. "Humans Have a Dark Fleet in Space." Video with Corey Goode on YouTube.

Reality Brief. "Spirituality inside of the Secret Space Programs." Video with Penny Bradley on YouTube.

Robert K. Rouse. "Half a Century of the German Moon Base (1942–1992)." Article on the VJ Enterprises website.

Michael Salla. "Corporate Bases on Mars and Nazi Infiltration of U.S. Secret Space Program." Article on the ExoPolitics website.

———. "Questions for Corey Goode about Temporal Drives, Galactic League of Nations Secret Space Program and Recent Controversy—8/4/15." Article on the ExoPolitics website.

———. "Questions for Corey Goode on SSP Conflicts and Human Slave Trade—May 29–30, 2015." Article on the ExoPolitics website.

———. "Secret Space Programs More Complex than Previously Revealed." Article on the ExoPolitics website.

Michael Shore. "The Illuminati Always Win the 'Election.'" Article on the Biblioteca Pleyades website.

Super Soldier Talk with James Rink. "Penny Bradley—SSP Dark Fleet Pilot." Video on YouTube.

———. "Kevan Trimmel—Solar Warden Empath." Video on YouTube.

UAMN TV. "Secret Space Program Whistleblowers Claim We Have Technology 1,000 Years Ahead of Anything You See." Video of Frank Chelli talk at Mutual UFO Network event, on YouTube.

Bibliography

Boysen, Earl, and Nancy Boysen. *Nanotechnology for Dummies.* 2nd ed. Indianapolis: Wiley Publishing, 2011.

Dorsey, Herbert G., III. *The Covert Colonization of Our Solar System.* Parker, Colo.: Outskirts Press, 2017.

———. *Inside the Secret Space Programs.* Parker, Colo.: Outskirts Press, February 15, 2017.

———. *Secret Science and the Secret Space Program.* Parker, Colo.: Outskirts Press, 2017.

Farrell, Joseph P. *The Nazi International: The Nazis' Postwar Plan to Control Finance, Conflict, Physics, and Space.* Kempton, Ill.: Adventures Unlimited Press, 2008.

———. *The Third Way: The Nazi International, European Union, and Corporate Fascism.* 1st ed. Kempton, Ill.: Adventures Unlimited Press, 2015.

Icke, David. *The Biggest Secret: The Book that Will Change the World.* 2nd updated ed. Ryde, United Kingdom: David Icke Books, 1999.

———. *And the Truth Shall Set You Free.* David Icke Books, 2004.

Kasten, Len. *Alien World Order: The Reptilian Plan to Divide and Conquer the Human Race.* Rochester, Vt.: Bear & Company, 2017.

Kaye, E. J. *This is the Dead Land.* Self-published, 2013. Novel about German crimes in Namibia.

Marvin, W. Meyer, and James M. Robinson. *The Nag Hammadi Scriptures: The Revised and Updated Translation of Sacred Gnostic Texts.* New York: Harper One, 2007.

O'Brien, Cathy, and Mark Phillips. *Trance Formation of America: The True Life Story of a CIA Mind Control Slave.* Rev. ed. Reality Marketing, Inc., 1995.

Olasuga, David, and Casper W. Erichsen. *The Kaiser's Holocaust: Germany's*

Forgotten Genocide and the Colonial Roots of Nazism. London: Faber & Faber Main Edition, 2011.

Salla, Michael E. *Antarctica's Hidden History: Corporate Foundations of Secret Space Programs.* Pahoa, Hawaii: Exopolitics Consultants, 2017.

———. *Insiders Reveal Secret Space Programs & Extraterrestrial Alliances.* Pahoa, Hawaii: Exopolitics Institute, 2015.

———. *Kennedy's Last Stand: Eisenhower, UFOs, MJ-12 & JFK's Assassination.* Pahoa, Hawaii: Exopolitics Consultants, 2013.

———. *The U.S. Navy's Secret Space Program & Nordic Extraterrestrial Alliance.* Pahoa, Hawaii: Exopolitics Consultants, 2017.

Daily East Oregonian (Pendleton, Ore.). "Entire Tribe Killed: Germans Exterminate Natives of South West Africa." September 6, 1905.

Tompkins, William Mills. *Selected by Extraterrestrials.* North Charleston, S.C.: CreateSpace Independent Publishing, 2015.

Von Braun, Wernher. *The Mars Project.* English ed. Urbana, Ill.: University of Illinois Press, 1953.

Wilhelm II, German Emperor. *The Kaiser's Memoirs.* New York and London: Harper & Brothers Publishers, 1922.

Zubrin, Robert, and Arthur C. Clarke. *The Case for Mars: The Plan to Settle the Red Planet and Why We Must.* New York: Free Press Division of Simon & Schuster, 1996 and 2011.

Index

Numbers in *italics* preceded by *pl.* indicate color insert plate numbers.